Guitar for Seniors
by Mike Christiansen

Photos by M. K. Gaydos-Gabriel

Online Audio   www.melbay.com/99989BCDEB

D1476492

Audio Contents

1	Tuning	21	Oh, Sinner Man	41	Exercise (p. 52)	61	Jingle Bells	83	Exercise (p. 99)
2	Brother John	22	Exercise (p. 38)	42	Tom Dooley	62	Exercise (p. 70)	84	Merrily
3	Row, Row,	23	Rollin' In My Sweet	43	Oh, Suzanna	63	Exercise (p. 70)		We Roll Along
	Row Your Boat		Baby's Arms	44	Kum Ba Yah	64	Home on the Range	85	Song of Joy
4	Rock-A-My-Soul	24	Exercise (p. 39)	45	Exercise (p. 55)	65	My Wild Irish Rose	86	A Separate Peace
5	He's Got The Whole	25	When the Saints Go	46	Scarborough Fair	66	My Bonnie Lies	87	When the Saints
	World In His Hands		Marching In	47	America the		Over the Ocean		Go Marching In
6	Down in the Valley	26	Exercise (p. 41)		Beautiful	67	Exercise (p. 74)	88	Scarborough Fair
7	Exercise (p. 24)	27	Midnight Special	48	America	68	Mr. Bojangles	89	Malaga
8	Exercise (p. 25)	28	Exercise (p. 43)	49	Exercise (p. 58)	69	Exercise (p. 82)	90	A Poor Wayfaring
9	Marianne	29	Amazing Grace	50	Exercise (p. 59)	70	The Water is Wide		Stranger
10	Exercise (p. 26)	30	Exercise (p. 44)	51	House of the	71	Exercise (p. 84)	91	Hungarian Dance #4
11	Will the Circle Be	31	Silent Night		Rising Sun	72	Scarborough Fair	92	Greensleeves
	Unbroken?	32	Take Me Out	52	Flat Broke Blues	73	Exercise (p. 85)	93	Walkin' Blues
12	Exercise (p. 28)		To The Ball Game	53	Exercise (p. 64)	74	Silent Night	94	Exercise (p. 109)
13	Exercise (p. 29)	33	Exercise (p. 48)	54	Exercise (p. 65)	75	Exercise (p. 88)	95	House of the
14	Exercise (p. 30)	34	Exercise (p. 48)	55	Exercise (p. 66)	76	A Poor Wayfaring		Rising Sun
15	This Little Light	35	Shenandoah	56	Exercise (p. 66)		Stranger	96	Klezmer Tune
	of Mine	36	When Johnny Comes	57	Exercise (p. 67)	77	Worried Man Blues	97	O Come, O Come
16	Amazing Grace		Marching Home	58	Will the Circle	78	Exercise (p. 90)		Emmanuel
17	Exercise (p. 32)	37	Exercise (p. 51)		Be Unbroken?	79	Baby Don't Love Me	98	Waltz
18	This Train	38	Worried Man Blues	59	Exercise (p. 68)	80	You're the Cure	99	Twilight
19	Molly Malone	39	Exercise (p. 52)	60	She'll Be Comin'	81	Song of Joy		
20	Exercise (p. 36)	40	Exercise (p. 52)		'Round the Mountain	82	Exercise (p. 98)		

1 2 3 4 5 6 7 8 9 0

Visit us on the Web at www.melbay.com — E-mail us at email@melbay.com

Table of Contents

Preface

This is a beginning guitar method. The contents of this book present the fundamentals of playing guitar in a sequence making the material logical and easy to learn. The primary difference between this method and many others is that this book is written for seniors wanting to learn to play the guitar. While many would say that getting on in years is only a state of mind, the fact is that some of the body parts (including the eyes) don't function quite the same as they did in younger years. With this in mind, the font has purposely been enlarged. Care has been taken to select repertoire familiar and appealing to a more mature audience and attention has been given to the pacing of the material.

Beginning senior students are to be complimented for studying the guitar at this time in their life. It says a great deal about the person who is constantly exploring and learning. It's never too late to learn something new. In fact, the experiences of years make seniors some of the best students.

Parts of the Guitar

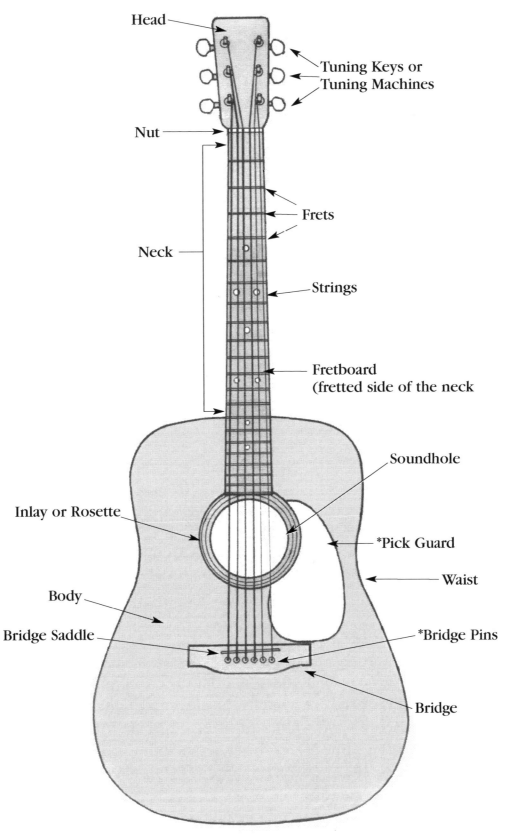

Head

Tuning Keys or
Tuning Machines

Nut

Frets

Neck

Strings

Fretboard
(fretted side of the neck

Soundhole

Inlay or Rosette

*Pick Guard

Waist

Body

Bridge Saddle

*Bridge Pins

Bridge

* This is not found on
the classical guitar.

Types of Guitars

Classic Guitar

This is an acoustic (non-electric) guitar. The classic guitar is characterized by the round sound hole, nylon or gut strings, and a rather wide neck. The reason for the wide neck is to allow the right-hand fingers to fit in between the strings for fingerstyle playing. The wood on a classic guitar is usually lighter than on a regular folk-style guitar in order to bring out the delicate tone of the nylon strings. Never put metal strings on a guitar made for nylon strings. The wood will not be able to stand the increased stress. We sometimes recommend starting on nylon strings, as they are easier (less painful) on the fingers.

Standard Flattop Guitar

This is a widely used guitar today. It is an acoustic guitar which may be played with the fingers or with a pick. It is characterized by steel strings and a narrower neck than is found on the "classic"-type guitars. The narrow neck makes it easier to finger barre chords or more complicated chords. This type of guitar puts out considerably more volume than a nylon-string or classical guitar. We recommend using light or extra light gauge strings for beginning students.

Jumbo Folk Guitar

This style of guitar is similar to the standard flattop guitar except for the larger body. While the large body on this type of guitar is bulkier to handle, it produces a fuller and deeper tone. Some flattop guitars come with a wide neck to facilitate fingerstyle performance.

Twelve-String Guitar

The 12-string guitar has a large body which is similar to a jumbo model. The neck is wider in order to comfortably fit all 12 strings. The guitar is played like a regular 6-string model since the strings are tuned to the same notes. On a 12-string guitar there are six sets of strings, two strings to a set. Each set is tuned to the corresponding set on a 6-string guitar; however, the 3rd, 4th, 5th, and 6th sets have an octave spread. While this style of guitar is excellent for folk and blues playing, it is bulkier and less mobile technically. It is not recommended, therefore, that a student begin with this type of guitar.

Arch-Top

This type of guitar gets its name from the curved (arched) top on the instrument. Both the front and back of this type of guitar are arched. Modern arch-top guitars usually contain "F"-shaped sound holes. The curvature of the front and back lend a degree of mellowness to the sound. The "F" holes tend to project the sound for a greater distance than a comparable round-hole model. Arch-type guitars find much usage as rhythm instruments in dance bands and in country music. Most folk and fingerstyle players prefer the immediate full spread of sound found on round-hole models. Arch-top guitars have metal strings and are usually played with an electric pick-up.

Solid-Body Electric

This is the type of guitar found in most of today's rock and blues music. It is built for speed and amplification. The sound possibilities are endless, depending on the pick-up, tone, and amplifier combination chosen.

Hollow-Body Electric

This type of guitar is also found in much of today's popular music. Again, the sound possibilities vary according to the electric components selected. Many jazz guitarists prefer an acoustic electric with a deep body (essentially, this is an arch-top guitar with an electric pick-up mounted on it). A mellow tone can result from this combination, but the type of electrical pick-up and amplifier influence this.

Acoustic Electric

This is an acoustic guitar (nylon or steel string) which has been equipped with a pick-up so it can be plugged into an amplifier. This type of guitar may be played unamplified or amplified.

Buying a Guitar

When buying a guitar there are several qualities of a good instrument that should be considered.

Type of guitar:

As shown in the previous section of this book, there are many types of guitars. For most beginning players, it is suggested they use the classical guitar or the steel-string acoustic. The classical guitar, with its nylon strings, will be easier on the fingertips. The steel-string acoustic has a narrower neck than the classical and may make some fingerings easier. In the early stages of learning to play the guitar, any style of music can be played on either guitar. Decide which guitar you like the feel and sound of the best. Guitars come in many sizes. It is important to get a guitar which feels comfortable to you. It should not feel too large or too small.

Price:

The prices of guitars vary greatly. Generally, you get what you pay for. Solid-top guitars (those in which the top of the guitar is one piece of wood thick) are a bit more expensive, but generally have a better tone and sound louder. Of course, hand-made guitars are more expensive, but they will play better and sound better.

Woods:

The tops of most guitars are made of cedar or spruce. Cedar tops usually sound mellower; whereas, the spruce tops sounds a bit brighter. The sides and backs are usually made of mahogany or rosewood. Mahogany guitars often sound more mellow and make good rhythm instruments. Guitars with rosewood backs and sides usually provide more versatility and work well for rhythm or solo playing.

Straight neck:

Make sure the neck on the guitar is straight. Sight down the neck as though looking down an arrow. Make sure the neck does not bend. Steel-string guitars may be adjusted, but it is much harder to change any bow in the neck on nylon string guitars. The straightness of the neck may also be checked by first, touching the sixth string (the largest string) in the first fret. Then, while pressing down the sixth string in the first fret with a left-hand finger, press the same string in one of the very high frets (like the fourteenth fret) with a right-hand finger. The string should be flush with the neck in the middle. If there is a lot of clearance in the middle of the neck between the string and the neck, the neck is bent. A very small amount of clearance is common and even desired on some guitars.

Grain on the top:

Try to get a guitar in which the wood grain on the top runs straight. If the grain is wider on the top and the bottom, and gets closer towards the middle of the guitar, generally the instrument will have a balanced tone. Wide-grained guitars have more bass response, and narrow grained guitars have more treble response.

Color:

When comparing several guitars of the same brand and model, generally, the guitar with the darkest top will have the best sound. This is not true when comparing different brands or models.

Tuning gears: Make sure the tuning gears are not too loose, but are not so tight that they do not turn easily.

Pitch:

The body of each guitar is designed so it will respond louder when certain notes are played. This can be checked by tuning the guitar and humming into the sound hole. Hum high and drop in pitch until the loudest note is found. Then, find which note on the guitar is the note that matched the note responding loudest to the humming. Guitars that are tuned to G or A or E are highly desired because those notes are commonly played on the acoustic guitar.

Case:

Get a case that will protect your guitar from the elements. Hard-shell cases are better than cardboard. But, a cardboard case is better than no case at all. Do not buy a case that is almost as expensive as the guitar.

Care of the Guitar

One of the most important actions that can be taken to protect the guitar is to get a case. There is a wide range in price in guitar cases. If one travels considerably, a more durable case is preferred. Hard-shell cases provide more protection than cardboard. Do not get a case that is too nice for the guitar. The nicer the guitar, the better the case should be.

If the guitar is in a very dry climate, use a guitar humidifier. These can be purchased at any music store. If the woods on the guitar are allowed to dry out, the woods may crack.

Polish the guitar. Guitar finishes like to be polished. Not only does polishing make the instrument look better, but it also protects the finish. Use a high quality guitar polish.

Avoid rapid temperature changes. Quickly taking the guitar from a hot environment to a cold one can damage the finish and/or the woods.

Use the proper strings. Classical guitars are to be strung with nylon strings and the steel-string acoustics are strung with steel strings. They should not be interchanged. Beginning players should use normal-tension nylon strings and light-gauge steel strings. A reputable music dealership can advise you on which brands to use. The strings should be replaced if: they are breaking, they are very discolored, they sound dull, they are very difficult to keep in tune.

Holding Position

When holding the guitar, it is important to be comfortable. To begin, hold the guitar with the waist of the guitar on the right leg and the neck facing left, as shown in the photo on the left. This position should be used to learn the material in this book even if the student is left-handed. This is the *folk* or *jazz position*. Both feet should remain flat on the floor.

For some, it may be more comfortable if the right foot is elevated. This can be done using a guitar stool (available at any music store). The neck of the guitar should be on a slight angle upward. Be careful not to hunch over the body of the guitar.

The holding position shown in the picture above on the right is the holding position used to play classical guitar. Notice, the guitar is held on the left leg with the leg elevated using a footstool. For now, use the holding position shown in the picture above on the left.

Right Hand

To avoid confusion of the left-hand and right-hand fingers, the right-hand fingers are labeled with letters. The letters come from the Spanish naming of the right-hand fingers.

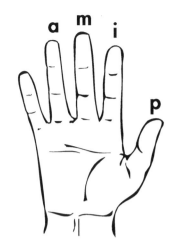

> *Right hand:*
>
> **p** = **pulgar** (thumb)
>
> **i** = **indice** (index finger)
>
> **m** = **media** (middle finger)
>
> **a** = **anular** (third finger)

The right arm is brought over the body of the guitar and touches near the elbow. Be careful not to touch too much of the top of the guitar with the right arm as this will dampen the tone. The right-hand fingers should be slightly curled and may lightly touch the top of the guitar just below the strings. Extend the right-hand thumb and rest it on the first (the smallest) string. For now, only the right-thumb will be used. Holding position of the pick will be presented later.

Stroke the first string several times. Be sure to use a downward motion combining movement of the wrist and elbow. The joint in the middle of the thumb should not bend.

Next, play the second string. After the thumb plucks the second string, it should come to rest on the first string. Repeat this process on each string. After the single string is picked, the thumb should come to rest on the string below it.

After playing the strings separately, rest the right-hand thumb on the second string and stroke strings two and one. Drop the thumb quickly so the strings sound simultaneously. Repeat this process with strings one, two, and three…then play the first four strings…then the first five strings, and finally all six strings. This action of playing more than one string is called *strumming*. Be sure to go straight down and use a combination of the right hand elbow, wrist, and thumb.

11

Left Hand

The left-hand finger numbers are shown on the illustration shown here.

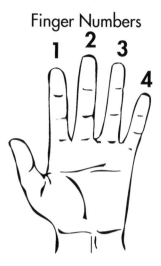

Finger Numbers
1 2 3 4

Left-Hand Position

The left hand is placed with the thumb on the back of the neck almost straight up and down. Be careful not to place the thumb over the top of the neck. Do not bend the thumb joint.

The thumb should be between the first and second fingers on the opposite side of the neck. The knuckles of the fingers should be very close to being parallel with the neck. When a left-hand finger is placed on a string, the tip of the finger should be used. The fingernails have to be very short. The knuckles of the finger should be square. The tip of the finger should be placed just behind (to your left) and next to the fret wire. The finger should not be on top of the fret wire. If the finger is too low in the fret, a dull sound will result. Enough pressure has to be applied to get a clear sound. Place the second finger in the second fret on the first string. Don't apply pressure. While picking the string repeatedly, gradually apply pressure until a clear tone is heard. This is how much pressure needs to be applied. No more…no less.

Tuning

There are several methods that can be used to tune the guitar. One of the easiest and most accurate is to use an electric tuner. Electric tuners can be purchased at any music dealership and are safe and easy to use. Some have built-in microphones and some attach to the guitar (not permanently). Those that attach to the guitar are useful because they leave your hands free, and the tuner will not pick up a lot of sounds other than your guitar. The guitar can also be tuned to a piano. The chart below shows the strings on the guitar and the corresponding pitches to which they would be tuned on the piano.

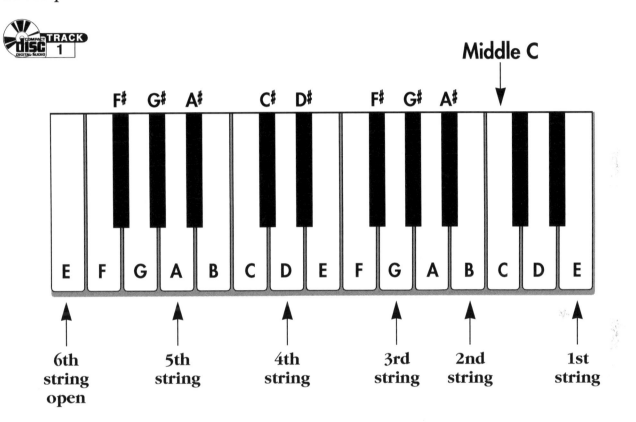

One of the simplest and most effective ways to tune a guitar is to tune the guitar to itself. If you have a piano or a pitch pipe, tune the first string of the guitar to E above middle C (see fig. 2). Then put a finger in the **fifth fret** on the **second string** and pick the second and the first strings together; they should sound the same (fig. 1). If they do not, adjust the string which has a finger on it until the two strings match in pitch.

When the second string is in tune, place a finger in the **fourth fret** on the **third string**. Pick the third and the second strings together. If they do not sound the same, adjust the third string which is the string with a finger on it. When these two strings sound the same, match the fourth string to the third by placing a finger in the **fifth fret** on the **fourth string** and match it to the third string open. The proces is then repeated in the **fifth fret** on the **fifth string** and matching it to the fourth string. Put a finger on the **sixth string** in the **fifth fret** and match it to the fifth string open (see fig. 3).

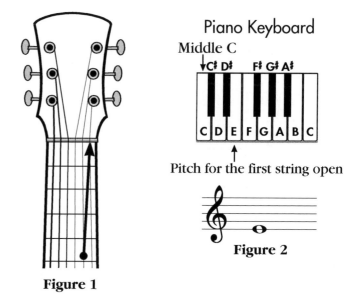

Pitch for the first string open

Figure 2

Figure 1

After all of this is done, strum several chords and see if the chords sound in tune. If they don't sound quite right, repeat the process and if it still does not help, something may be wrong with the instrument itself. The frets may be misplaced or the bridge of the guitar may need some adjusting. If so, take the instrument to a qualified repairman or to an instructor and let him adjust the instrument.

You may also tune each string on the guitar to pitches on the piano. If this method is used, then tune the first string open (without any fingers on the string) to E above middle C on the piano. The second string is tuned to B just below middle C. The third string to G below that B. The fourth string to a D. The fifth string to A and the sixth string is tuned to E (see fig. 4).

The guitar may also be tuned to a tuning fork. E tuning forks may be purchsed. Tap the tuning fork and touch it on the bridge of the guitar. The sound which resonates will be the pitch you match to the first string.

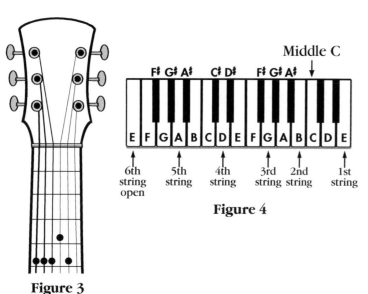

Figure 4

Figure 3

First Warm Up

To become familiar with the feel of the guitar, and to develop coordination, do the following warm-up exercise:

Step 1
Begin by playing the first string open. Open means no left-hand fingers are pushing on the string.

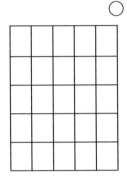

Step 2
Next, play the first string, first fret. The left-hand first finger should be pushing on the string. Be sure to get a good, clear sound.

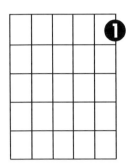

Step 3
Next, play the first string, second fret. The left-hand second finger should be used to push on the second fret.

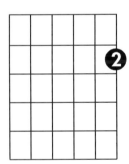

Step 4
Next, play the first string, third fret, using the left-hand third finger.

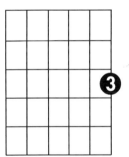

Step 5
Finally, play the first string, fourth fret, using the left-hand fourth finger.

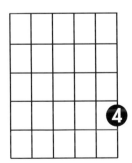

Now, play these same notes in reverse order (4-3-2-1), still on the first string. Repeat this exercise several times up and down the fingerboard. Notice that the same number left-hand finger is used as the fret number. After doing the exercise several times on the first string, repeat the same sequence on each string.

Reading Neck Diagrams

Drawn below is a diagram of the guitar neck. These diagrams are commonly used to illustrate the fingerings for chords. A chord is when three or more strings are played. The vertical lines represent the strings, with the first string to the far right. The horizontal lines represent the frets; the first fret is at the top of the diagram. The dots represent where to place left-hand fingers. The numbers on the dots indicate which left-hand finger to use. The circles above the diagram indicate open strings to be played. Open strings are those that do not have left-hand fingers pressing on them. An "X" above a string on the diagram indicates that that string is not to be played.

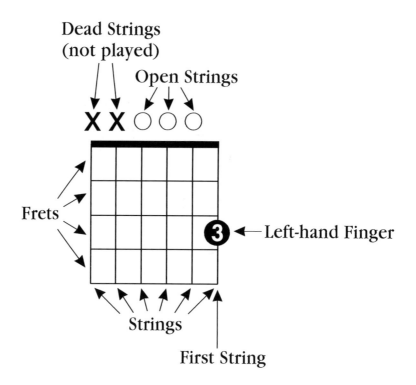

First Chords

The first chord to be presented is the simple G chord. As shown on the diagram below, this chord is played by placing the left-hand, third finger on the first string in the third fret. Four strings are strummed on this chord. As you can see, strings two, three, and four are played open. The first string is played, and strings five and six are not played. Strum this chord down several times.

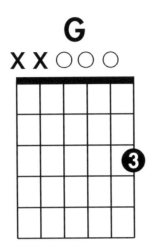

These two signs (✓ and ⸁) are called strum bars. They indicate to strum a chord down one time. Each strum bar gets one beat. Be sure to use a straight downward motion using the right-hand thumb.

Practice the following exercise strumming the G chord the number of times indicated by the strum bars. After strumming the G chord four times, play four strings open.

G **Open strings** **G** **Open strings**

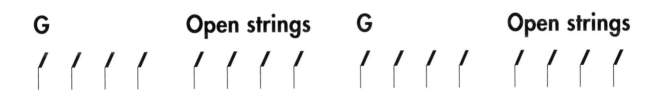

The following song can be accompanied by strumming only one chord…G. Play the G chord one time for each strum bar and sing the melody. Some strums do not have a word underneath and sometimes there are two syllables to a strum bar.

BROTHER JOHN

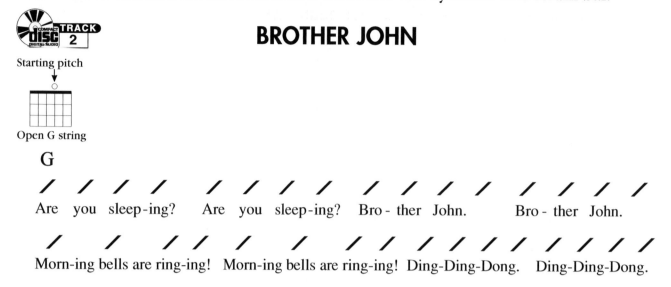

G

Are you sleep-ing?   Are you sleep-ing? Bro - ther John.   Bro - ther John.

Morn-ing bells are ring-ing! Morn-ing bells are ring-ing! Ding-Ding-Dong.   Ding-Ding-Dong.

The next chord to be learned is the C chord shown here. Practice playing the C chord several times.

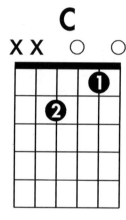

The next song uses only the C chord. Strum the C chord down one time for every strum bar. Keep the strums even. Be sure to strum the chord when the word under the strum bar is sung.

ROW, ROW, ROW YOUR BOAT

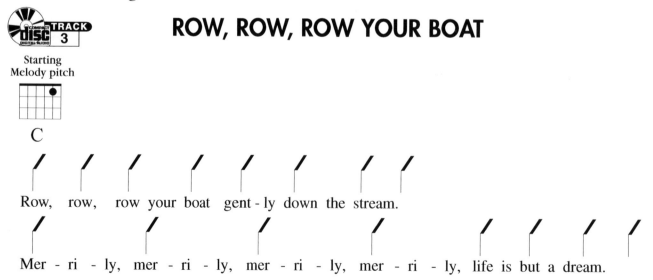

C

Row,   row,   row your boat gent - ly down the stream.

Mer - ri - ly, mer - ri - ly, mer - ri - ly, mer - ri - ly, life is but a dream.

The next exercise and song use the G and C chords. Practice changing the chords quickly and smoothly. To reach the point where the chords can be changed quickly, change from one chord to the next and keep the right hand strumming. Eventually, the right hand will force the left hand to change quickly.

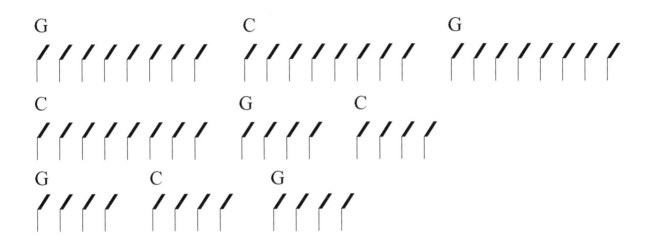

ROCK-A-MY SOUL

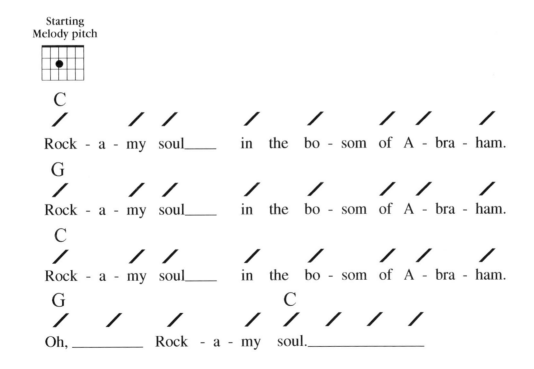

The next chord to learn is G7 shown below. Practice strumming this chord several times. Practice the song after the exercise. The song contains the C and G7 chords. Strum each chord one time for each strum bar.

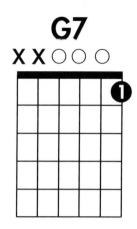

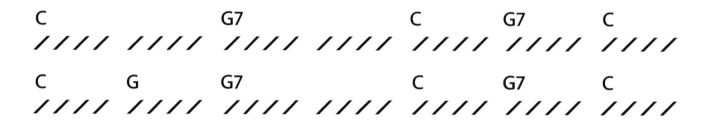

HE'S GOT THE WHOLE WORLD IN HIS HANDS

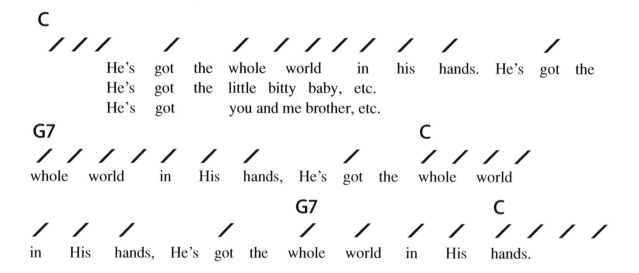

Rhythm Sheets

A *rhythm sheet* is a type of music that shows the lyrics to a song, the chords above the lyrics and a fraction at the beginning of the song (i.e. 4/4 or 3/4) called a time signature. Only be concerned with the top number in the *time signature*. The top number indicates how many times to strum each chord name. For example, in "Down in the Valley," because the top number in the time signature is a three, strum each chord name three times. Use only down strums.

DOWN IN THE VALLEY

C		C	C	C	G7	G7

3/4
1. Down in the val - ley   valley so low.   Hang your head
2. Build me a cas - tle   forty feet high.   So I can
3. Write me a let - ter.   Send it by mail.   Send it in

G7	G7	G7		C	C

o - ver.   Hear the wind   blow.
see him   as he rides   by.
care of   Birming - ham   jail.

Plectrums

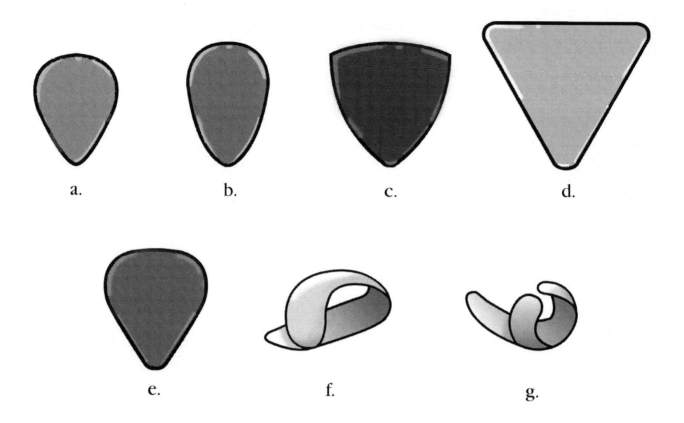

a.   b.   c.   d.

e.   f.   g.

Picks come in many shapes and thicknesses. It is suggested that beginning students use the medium size and medium thickness pick (fig. e). Large and thick picks are hard to control. They seem to grab when stroking the string rather than bend with the stroke. The smaller and larger picks (fig. a, fig. d) may be hard to control. The thick picks are becoming more popular because you cannot only pick softly with them, but they can be used to pick harder and produce more volume than the thin picks. Finger and thumb picks produce a very brilliant tone. The beginning student will find them hard to control. The thumb (fig. f) and finger (fig. g) picks are used primarily in folk music and are not recommended for beginning students.

Holding the Pick

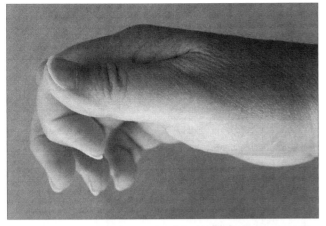 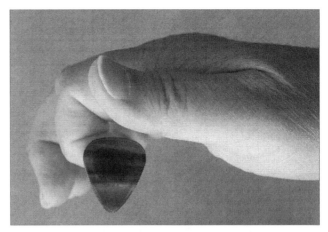

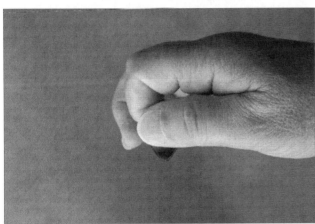 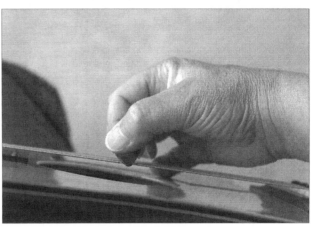

Picks (or plectrums) are commonly used when playing guitar. They may be used to play the nylon-string guitar as well as the steel string. The pick is held between the right-hand thumb and the index finger. The pick should be aimed toward the string. The index finger should be bent slightly more that the second, third, and fourth fingers. The fourth finger may lightly touch the top of the guitar, but should not be fixed. Be careful not to hold the pick too tightly, but hold it tightly enough to keep it from turning when the strings are played. When picking a single string or strumming, the pick should be tilted slightly forward and also tilted up slightly. When the pick passes over the strings, the pick should glide across the strings rather than snag them. The strumming and/or picking motion should be done using a combination of the movement of the right-hand wrist and the right elbow.

With the exception of the section on fingerstyle, when playing the material in this book, the pick may be used, or the right-hand thumb (without a pick) may be used. Remember, if the thumb is used, keep the right-hand fingers (1–4) curled as though holding a soft ball. When playing with the thumb, the movement should come from the right-hand wrist and the right elbow.

Measured Music

The five lines and four spaces in standard notation music is called a staff. Guitarists usually only read music that has a treble clef sign (ϕ) at the beginning of the music. The staff is divided into sections with bar lines. The sections between the bar lines are called measures. Inside of each measure, there are a specific number of beats. A beat is the pulse of the music or a measurement of time. Next to the treble clef sign is a fraction called a time signature. The top number in the time signature indicates how many beats are in each measure. The bottom number will be discussed later.

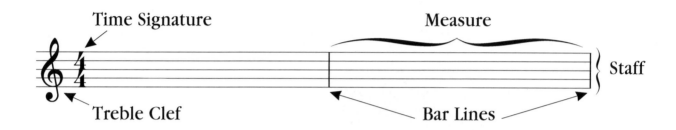

When playing rhythm guitar (the chords) for accompaniment, strum the chord written above the measure once for each beat in the measure. Strum down with the right-hand thumb. In 4/4 time, strum down four times in each measure. In 3/4 time, strum down three times in each measure. If a C is written where the time signature would appear, this stands for 4/4 or common time. If ¢ is written, this is cut time (2/2) and the chords should be strummed two times in each measure.

Practice the following exercises and songs strumming down in the measures.

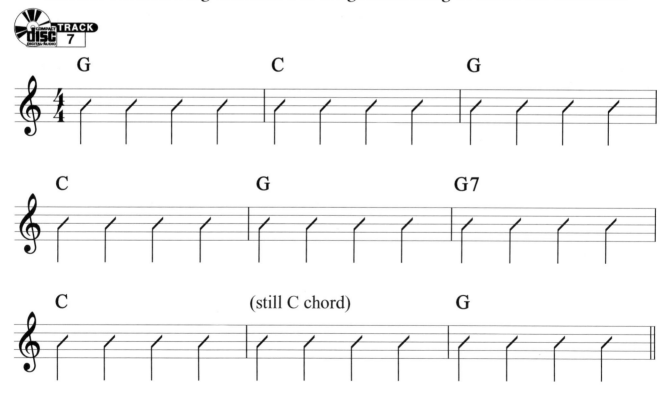

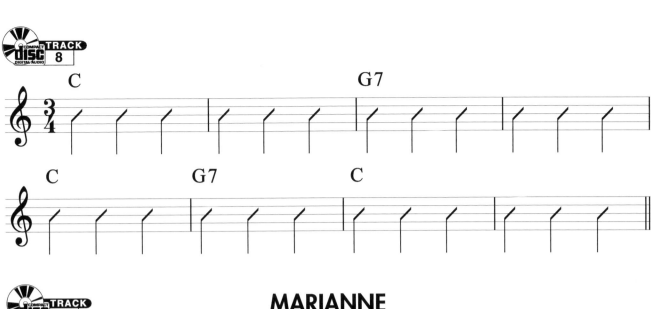

MARIANNE

Reminder to strum four times in a measure.

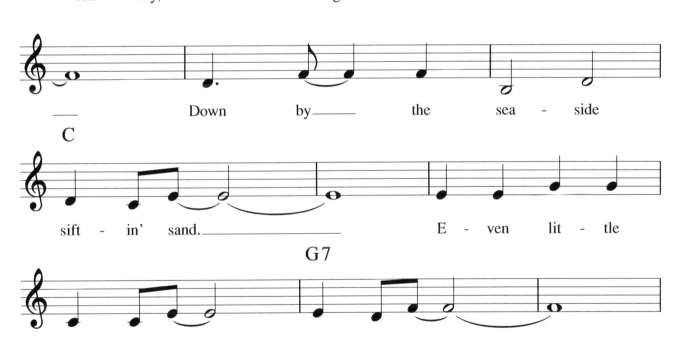

All day, ____ all night____ Mar - i - anne,_____

____ Down by_____ the sea - side

sift - in' sand._____ E - ven lit - tle

child - dren love____ Mar - i - anne,_____

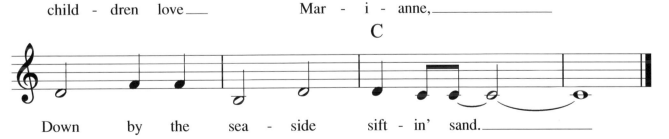

Down by the sea - side sift - in' sand._____

25

Full Chords

The following diagrams show many of the popular full chords. They are referred to as full chords because more strings may be strummed than the simpler versions of these chords presented earlier. Play the following exercises and songs using the full G, G7 and C chords. Use the same D chord that was presented earlier in the book. Strum each measure using the pattern shown above the first measure. Use down strums only and change the chords quickly. Some of these chords may seem quite difficult at first. Have patience and stick with it.

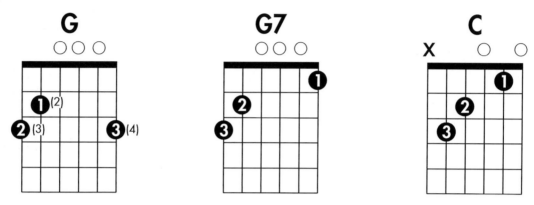

Practice the following exercises using full chords:

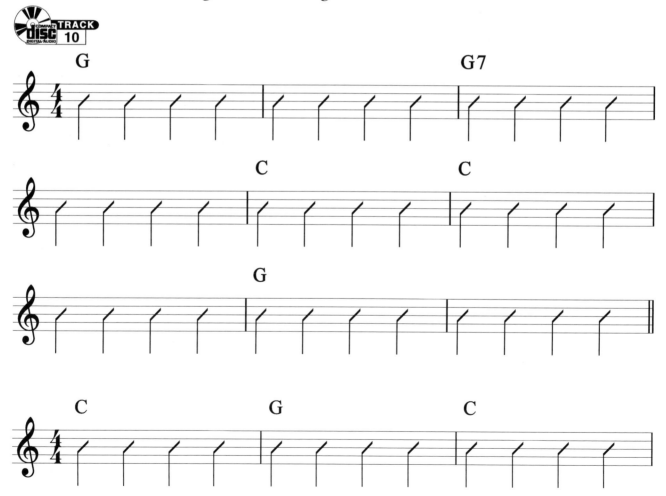

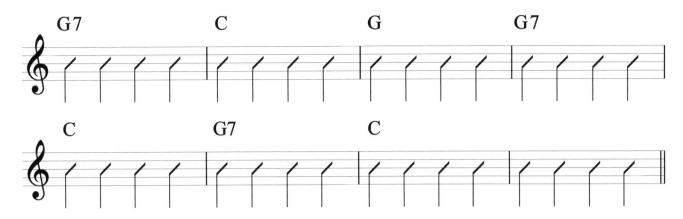

Practice the following songs using down strums and full chords. After playing this song, go back to the earlier songs in the book and substitute the full G, G7, and C chords for the simple chords of the same names. When playing the chords, do not be concerned with the notes (♩♩♩) but rather only the chord written above the measures, how many beats are in a measure, and how many measures the chord gets. The notes are the melody to be sung. If a song begins with pickup notes (notes in an incomplete measure at the beginning), sing the pickup notes and begin strumming in the first complete measure.

WILL THE CIRCLE BE UNBROKEN?

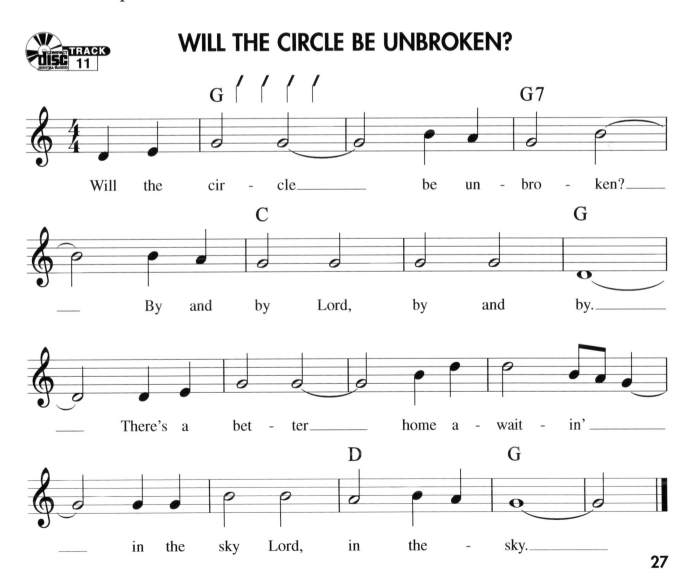

The D Chord

The chord drawn below is a D chord. The first three fingers of the left hand are used and four strings are strummed.

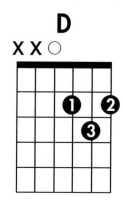

Practice the following exercise that contains a D chord.

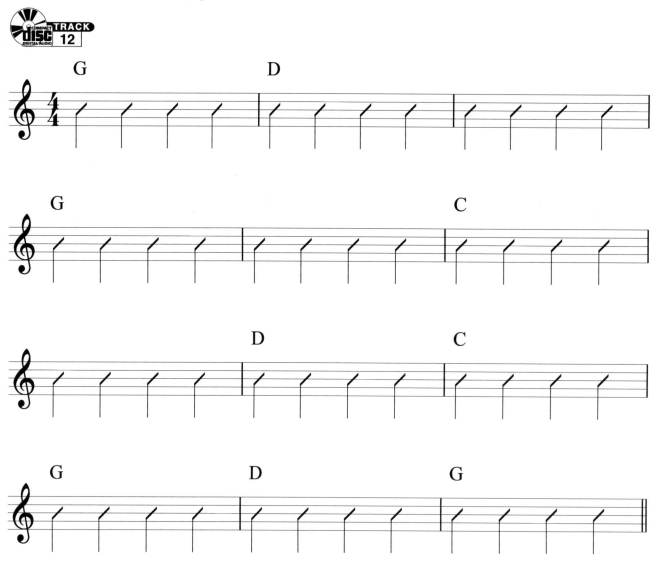

The E minor Chord

The chord drawn below is an E minor chord. Minor chords are written with an "m" next to the chord letter name. The E minor chord uses the left-hand second and third fingers. All six strings may be strummed.

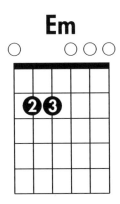

Practice the following exercises containing the E minor chord.

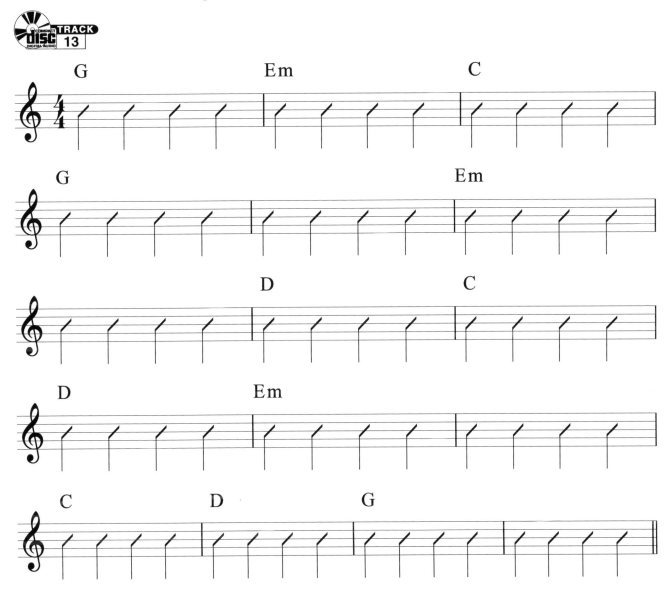

A *chord progression* is a series of chords. The following chord progression contains an E minor chord and is commonly found in Spanish music.

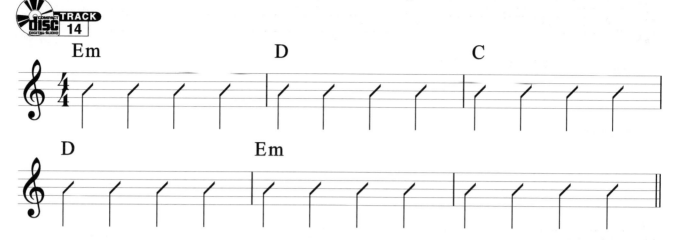

Practice the following songs that contain the chords presented so far. If the song is in 4/4, strum down four times in a measure. If the song is in 3/4, strum down three times in each measure.

THIS LITTLE LIGHT OF MINE

let it shine, ___ let it shine. ___

AMAZING GRACE

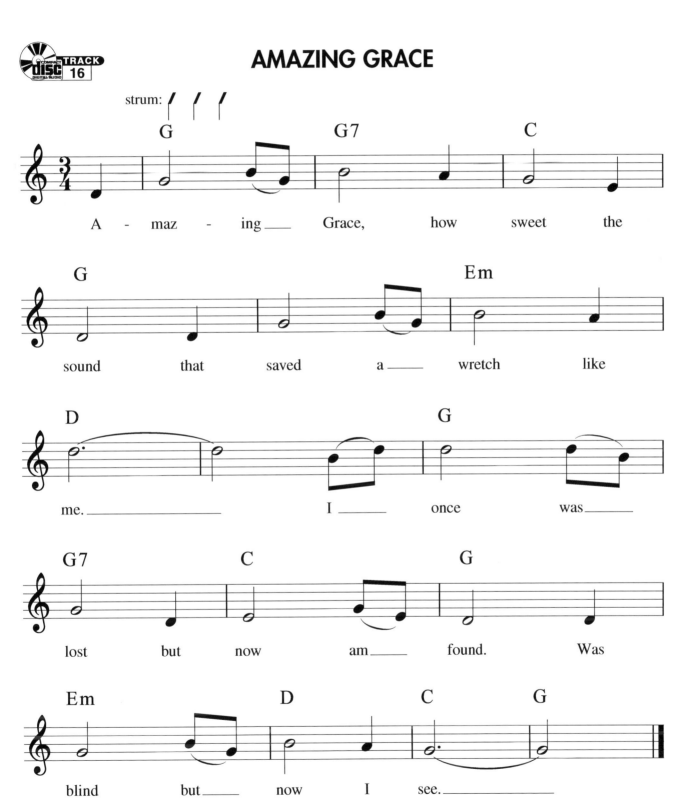

A - maz - ing ___ Grace, how sweet the

sound that saved a ___ wretch like

me. ___ I ___ once was ___

lost but now am ___ found. Was

blind but ___ now I see. ___

Two New Chords

Drawn below are the Am and D7 chords. Practice them individually and then play the exercise and songs containing these new chords. Notice when changing from a C chord to an Am chord, the left-hand first and second fingers remain in the same place. Also, when changing from Am or C to the D7 chord, the left-hand, first finger remains in the same position. Fingers that remain in the same place when chords change are called *pivot fingers*.

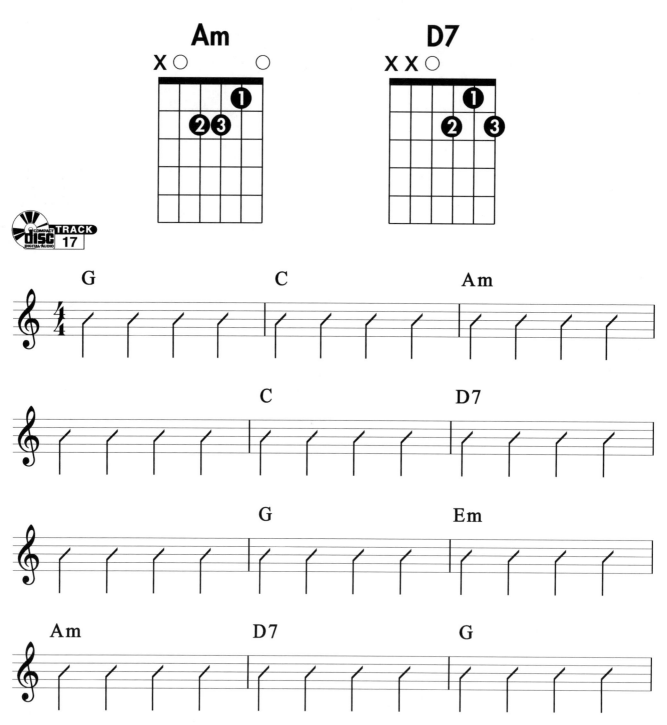

Whole note strum. Strum the chord on beat one and let it ring through beats two, three, and four.

THIS TRAIN

strum:

This train is bound for glo-ry, this train!

This train is bound for glo-ry,

This train! This train is bound for glo-ry,

don't take none but the good and Ho-ly. This train is

bound for glo-ry, this train!

MOLLY MALONE

Up Strum

When strumming a chord with an up stroke, regardless of the chord being played, only strum two or three strings. The up strum is executed with an up and outward motion. This sign, ⊓, above a strum bar, is used to indicate a down stroke. This sign, ⋁, is used to indicate an up stroke. Generally, when two strum bars are connected with a beam, there are two strums in one beat. The first comes on the first half of the beat and is played with a down stroke. The second is played on the second half of the beat and is played using an up stroke. The down stroke is counted as the beat on which it occurs, and the up stroke is counted as "and."

Practice the following exercise strumming each chord as indicated.

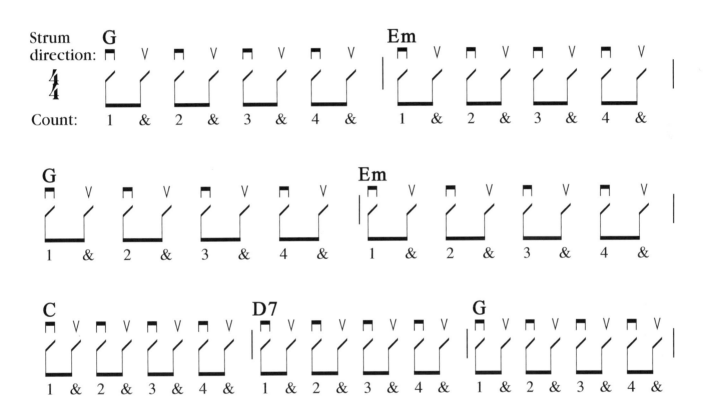

Strum Patterns for 4/4

The simplest strum pattern for 4/4 (strumming down four times in each measure) was presented earlier. The simplest strum pattern for 3/4 is to strum down three times in each measure. Although these patterns are easy to execute, when used in the right song, they can be effective. This section of the book will present several strum patterns that use combinations of down and up strums. By combining down and up strums, interesting accompaniment patterns can be created. An exercise and a song will be given to apply each strum pattern. Although an exercise and song are presented with each strum pattern, each pattern can be used to play any song in 4/4. The strum patterns presented in this section of the book can be applied to sheet music and songbooks as well as the songs and exercises in this book. Generally, once a pattern has been selected, the same pattern is used in each measure throughout the song.

The strum pattern written below takes one measure in 4/4 to complete. Reminders of the strum direction are written above the strum bars, and the rhythm is written below the strum bars. Hold any chord and practice this strum pattern.

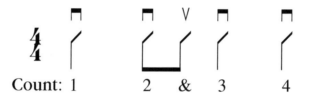

Count: 1   2   &   3   4

Practice the following exercises and song using the strum pattern written above or in the first measure. Use the same strum pattern written in or above the first measure to play every measure.

Repeat the previous strum pattern and chord in the empty measures.

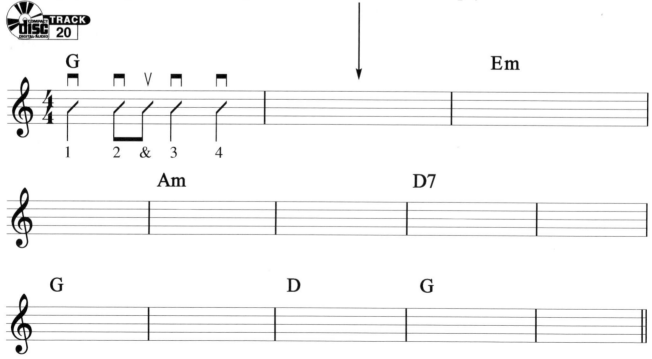

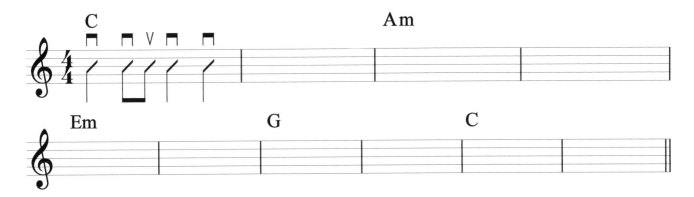

When playing the chords, do not be concerned with the notes, but rather the chords, how many beats are in each measure, and how many measures the chord gets. Use the same strum pattern in each measure.

OH, SINNER MAN

Spiritual

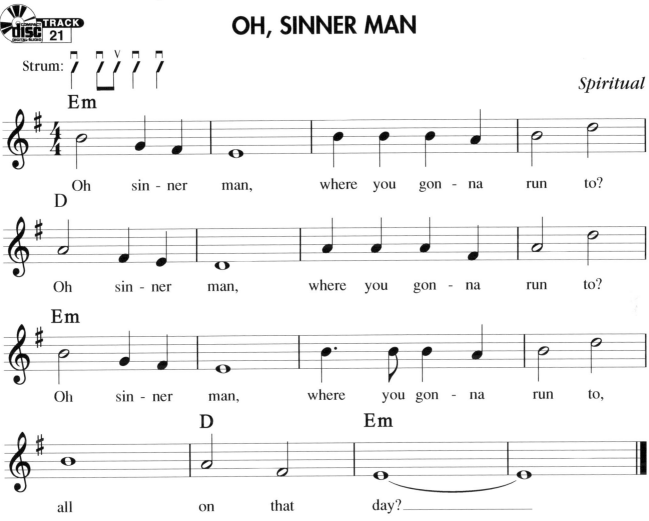

Written below is another strum that works to play songs in 4/4. After practicing the strum pattern holding any chord, apply the strum pattern to the exercise and song that follows.

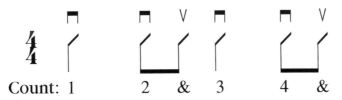

ROLL IN MY SWEET BABY'S ARMS

Well, I ain't gon - na work on the rail - road.

Ain't gon - na work on the farm. Gon - na

lay 'round this shack 'til the mail - train comes

back, then I'll roll in my sweet ba - by's arms.

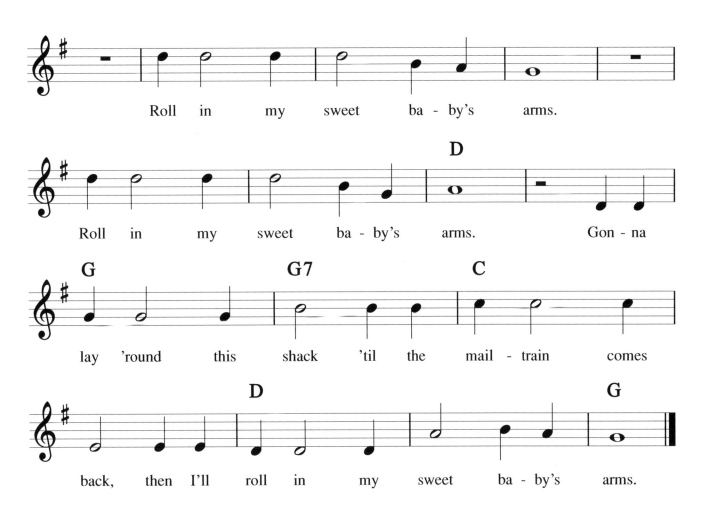

Roll in my sweet ba - by's arms.

Roll in my sweet ba - by's arms. Gon - na

lay 'round this shack 'til the mail - train comes

back, then I'll roll in my sweet ba - by's arms.

Here is another strum that works well for 4/4. Practice this strum pattern and the exercise and song.

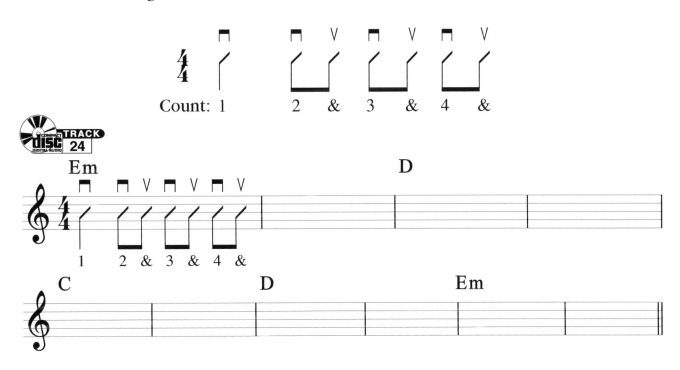

WHEN THE SAINTS GO MARCHING IN

A loop that connects two strum bars is called a *tie*. When the tie is written, play the strum bar at the left of the tie, but do not play the strum bar connected on the right side of the tie. Instead, allow the strum at the first of the tie to ring through the strum bar connected with the tie.

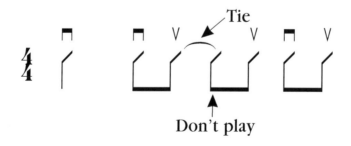

The following strum pattern can be used to play songs in 4/4. It is a bit tricky because of the tie. There are two up strums together in the middle of the pattern with a pause between them (where the other down strum would have been). Remember, when strumming up, play only two or three strings.

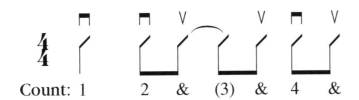

Count: 1   2   &   (3)   &   4   &

Practice the following exercise and songs using the strum pattern containing a tie.

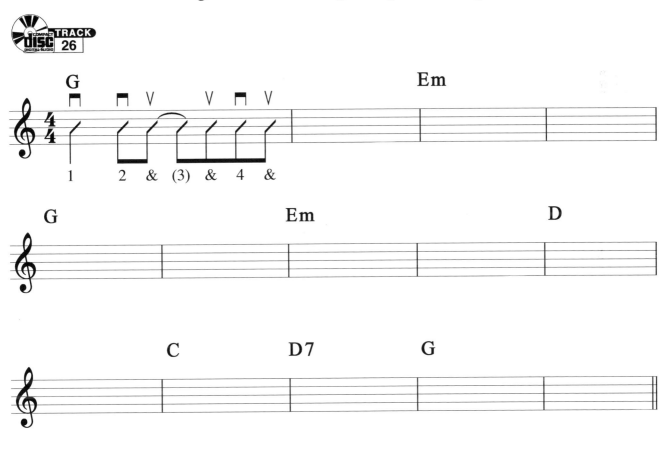

Repeat Sign

The song, "Midnight Special," contains a repeat sign. When a repeat sign, :||, is written, go from that spot in the music to where the repeat sign with the dots on the right, ||:, is written in the music and play that portion of the music again. The song may be repeated once or as many times as it takes to sing all of the verses. Practice strumming the following song.

MIDNIGHT SPECIAL BLUES

Unknown

Wake up in the morn - in' when the ding dong—

rings. March up to the____ ta - ble,

you see the same old things. Let the Mid - night

Spe - cial shine its light on____ me. Let the Mid - night

Spe - cial shine its ev - er lov - in' light on ____ me.

Repeat sign

Additional Verse:

2. There upon the table
   Knife and fork and pan,
   Say a word about it
   There's trouble with the man.

Strum Patterns for 3/4

The strum patterns in this section of the book can be used to play songs in 3/4. Each pattern is presented with an exercise and song. However, all of these patterns can be applied to any song in 3/4. Each pattern takes one measure to complete. Like the patterns for 4/4, once a pattern has been selected, use the same strum pattern in each measure. Also, like the 4/4 patterns, these patterns for 3/4 are listed in order of difficulty. Hold any chord at first while learning each pattern.

The following pattern contains one up strum. First, play the pattern holding any chord. Then, play the exercise and song.

AMAZING GRACE

A - maz - ing ___ Grace, how sweet the

sound that saved a ___ wretch like___

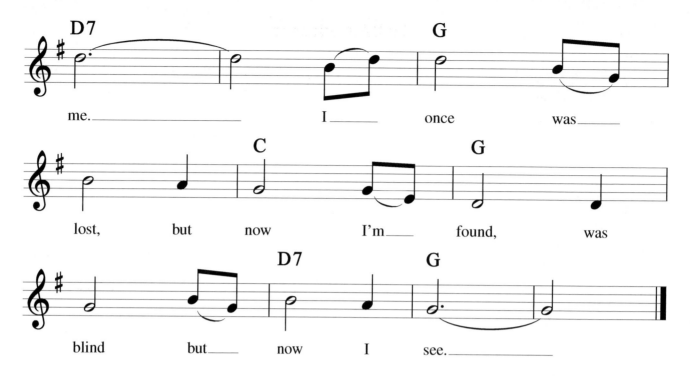

me. _____ I ___ once was ___

lost, but now I'm ___ found, was

blind but ___ now I see. _____

Here is another strum pattern for 3/4.

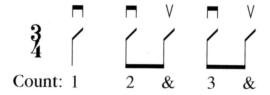

Count: 1   2 & 3 &

The next strum pattern for 3/4 contains two up strums. Hold any chord to learn the pattern. Then, practice the exercise below.

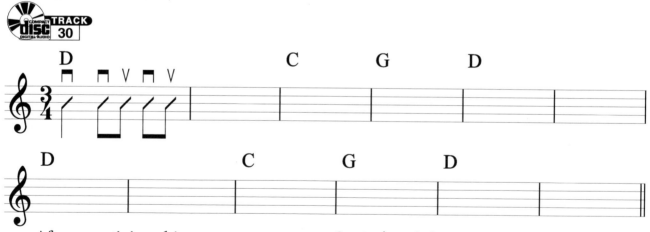

After practicing this new strum pattern for 3/4 and the following exercise, return to the songs presented earlier in this section of the book that used strum patterns for 3/4 and apply this new pattern to each measure.

Remember, the strum patterns for 4/4 and 3/4 can be applied to songs written in sheet music or songbooks. For now, play only songs that have no more than one chord per measure. Playing music in which there are two or more chords in a measure will be presented later.

SILENT NIGHT

Franz Grüber

Si - lent night, ho - ly night,

All is calm, all is bright. Round yon

vir - gin moth - er and child. Ho - ly in - fant so

ten - der and mild. Sleep in heav - en - ly

peace. _____ Sleep___ in heav - en - ly peace. _____

Additional Verse

2. Silent night, holy night,
   Shepherds quake at the sight.
   Glories stream from heaven afar,
   Heavenly hosts sing Alleluia;
   Christ the Savior is born!
   Christ the Savior is born!

New Chords: A7 and E7

Practice the A7 and E7 chords drawn on the diagrams below. Notice, there are two fingerings given for each chord. The fingering on the left is easier, but practice both of them. In the diagram of the A7 on the right, the loop over the top of the numbers indicates that the first finger lays across (or bars) strings two, three, and four. Play the exercise and songs containing these new chords. Any of the strum patterns for 3/4 may be used. Remember, once a pattern has been selected, use the same pattern to play each measure of the song.

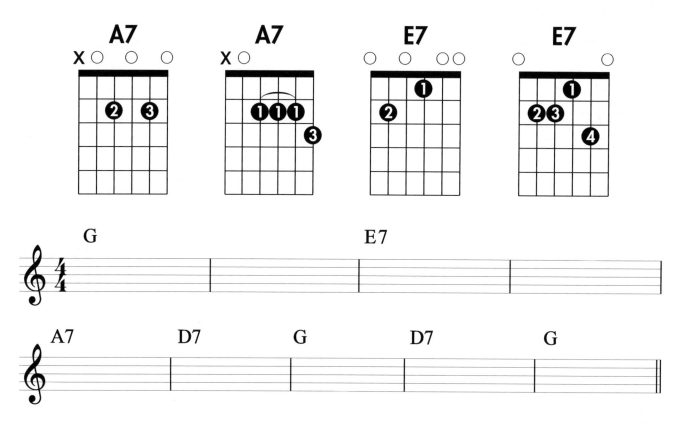

TAKE ME OUT TO THE BALLGAME

Words by Jack Norworth
Music by Albert Von Tilzer

G   D7

Take   me   out   to   the   ball

G

game;   take   me   out   with   the

crowd. _____ Buy me some

pea - nuts and Crack - er Jacks,

I don't care if I nev - er get

back. Let me root, root, root for the home

team; if they don't win, it's a shame. _____

This is a C#dim chord. →

C#dim   G

____ For it's one, two, three strikes, you're

out, at the old ball - game. _____

New Chords: Dm and Bm

Drawn on the diagrams below are the D minor and B minor chords. After practicing them individually, play the exercises and songs containing these two new chords. Use any of the previously learned strum patterns for 4/4 or 3/4.

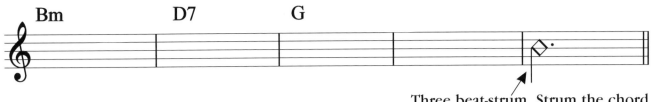

Three beat-strum. Strum the chord on the first beat and let it ring through the next two beats.

SHENANDOAH

Oh, Shen - an - doah, I long to hear you, a - way, _____ you roll - ing riv - er. _____ Oh Shen - an - doah, I long to hear you. A - way, _____ we're bound a - way, 'cross the wide Mis - sou - ri.

WHEN JOHNNY COMES MARCHING HOME

When John - ny comes march - ing home a - gain, Hur -

rah,_____ Hur - rah._____ When John - ny comes

march - ing home a - gain, Hur - rah,_____ Hur -

rah._____ The_____ men will sing and the

boys will shout; the la - dies they_____ will

all turn out, and we'll all be gay

when John - ny comes march - ing home._____

New Chords: A and E

Drawn here are the A and E chords. Practice changing the two chords back and forth, then practice the exercise and song which follow. Use any strum pattern for 4/4.

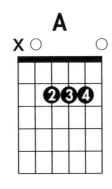

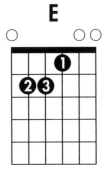

WORRIED MAN BLUES

Suggested strum pattern:

It takes a wor-ried man to sing a wor-ried song. It takes a wor-ried, wor-ried man to sing a wor-ried song. It takes a wor-ried man to sing a wor-ried song. I'm wor-ried now, but I won't be wor-ried long.

Playing Two Chords in a Measure

If you are playing the accompaniment and two chords appear in one measure in a song in 4/4, the strum pattern can be discontinued and each chord strummed down twice.

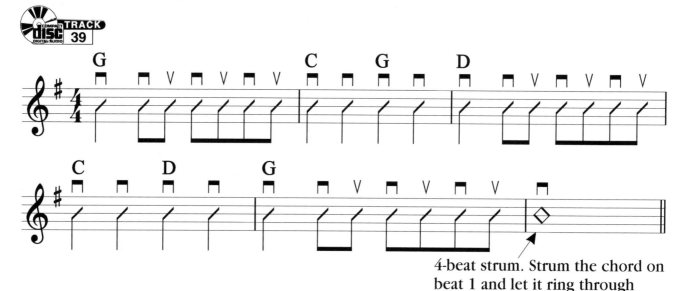

4-beat strum. Strum the chord on beat 1 and let it ring through beats 2–4.

If two chords appear in a measure in 3/4, see which chord gets the most space in that measure and strum that chord down twice and the other chord down once.

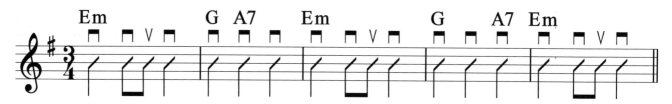

Play the following exercises and songs in which some measures contain two chords.

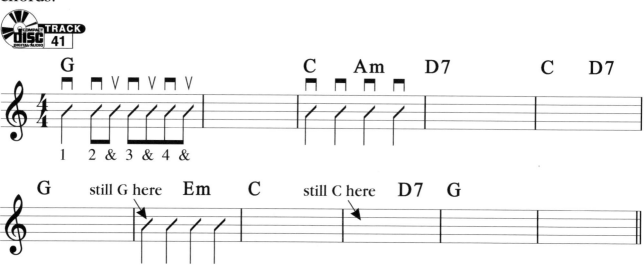

TOM DOOLEY

Traditional Cowboy Song

OH, SUZANNA

Stephen C. Foster

KUM BA YAH

African Spiritual

SCARBOROUGH FAIR

Old English Song

Are you go - ing to Scar - bor - ough Fair? Par - sley, sage, rose - ma - ry and thyme. Re - mem - ber me to one who lives there. ___ She once was a true love of mine.

AMERICA THE BEAUTIFUL

Katherine Lee Bates

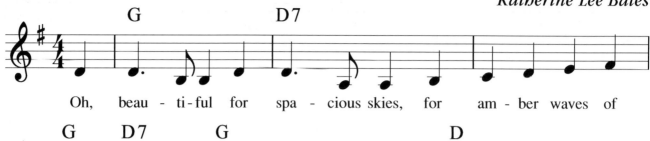

AMERICA

Henry Carey

56

From ev - 'ry___ moun - tain-side, let free - dom ring!

If more than two chords appear in a measure in 4/4, for now, eliminate all but the first and third chords in the measure and then apply the rule for two chords in a measure. In 3/4 time, if more than two chords appear in a measure, play only the first and second chords in the measure and eliminate the others.

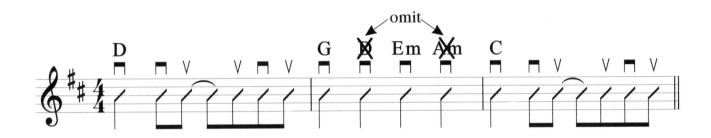

Another method of strumming two chords in a measure is to divide the strum patterns. The following examples show how this can be done. Notice when the pattern is used, the second chord in the measure is played on the first up strum (beat "2 and").

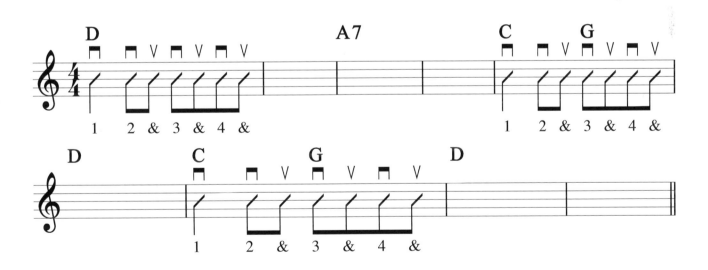

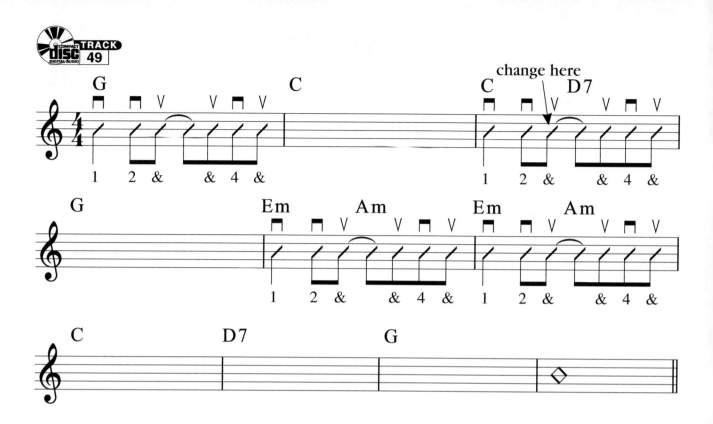

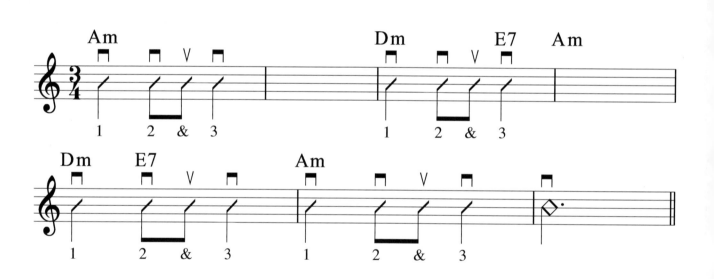

The B7 Chord

The B7 chord is drawn below. Practice this new chord and then the exercises and songs that follow. Use any of the previously learned strum patterns for 3/4 and 4/4.

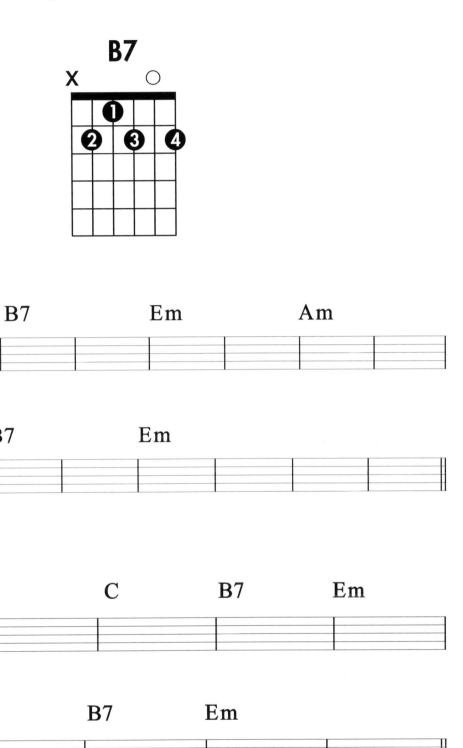

HOUSE OF THE RISING SUN

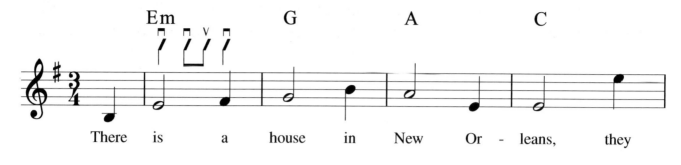

There is a house in New Or - leans, they

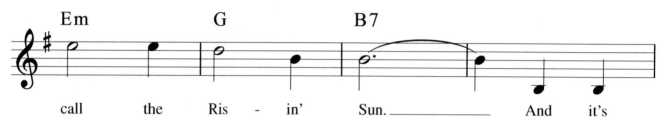

call the Ris - in' Sun. And it's

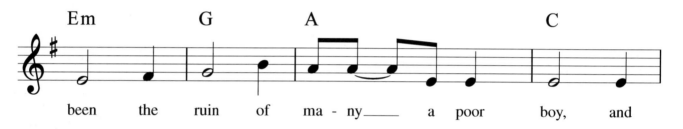

been the ruin of ma - ny a poor boy, and

yes, I know I'm one.

First and Second Endings

Occasionally in a song, a first and second ending appear (|1.___ |2.___). When this occurs, play the first ending and observe the repeat signs. Then, on the second time through, skip the first ending, play the second ending and continue. Sometimes the song will end with the second ending.

Play the following song that contains a first and second endings and the B7 chord.

FLAT BROKE BLUES

More Repeat Signs

When D.C. is written above a staff, go from that point in the music to the beginning of the music and play it again.

D.C. al Coda ⊕ means go to the beginning and play to where "to Coda ⊕" is written. Then, go from that point to "Coda ⊕," which is usually near the end of the piece. End after playing the coda (the ending). See example ① below.

When *D.S.* 𝄋 is written, go from that point in the music to where the D.S. sign (𝄋) is written earlier in the music and play the music until further directions are indicated.

D.S. al Fine means to repeat from that point to the D.S. sign and play to where "Fine" is written. End the music at "*Fine.*" Fine means to finish. See example ② on the following page.

If *D.S. al Coda* is written, go from that point in the music to the D.S. sign (𝄋). Then, play until "to Coda" ⊕ is written. After that, skip to the Coda (⊕) and play the coda (the ending). See example ③ on the following page.

Play the following exercises that contain these repeat signs. Use any one of the strum patterns for 4/4.

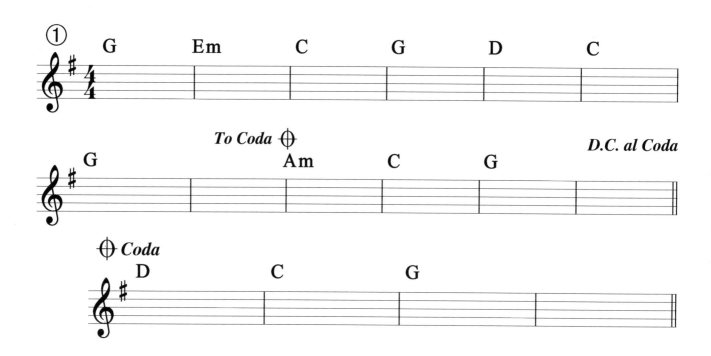

Alternating Bass

A type of accompaniment that is very popular on the guitar is *alternating bass*. This style of accompaniment is also referred to as alternating pick-strum, or Carter style. Alternating bass can be simple to learn and provides a great accompaniment for singers.

To learn this style, divide the chords you have learned into the following three categories: 1) 6-string chords (chords on which 6 strings may be strummed, like G and Em); 2) 5-string chords (chords on which 5 strings are strummed, like C and Am); and 3) 4-string chords (chords where 4 strings are strummed, like D and F).

The first alternating bass pattern to learn works for 4/4 time. The pattern takes one measure to complete. For one measure of a 6-string chord (such as G), the pattern is written below.

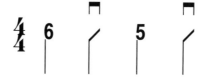

The numbers show the individual strings to pick. The picking of a single string is followed by a strum. The strums are down strums. Pick the sixth string, then strum the chord. This is followed by picking the fifth string and then strumming the chord. Each strum gets one beat, and each single-string pick gets one beat. The stems under the numbers are like the stems on quarter strum bars. They indicate that picking the single string takes one beat. The single strings may be picked with the right-hand thumb, and the strum may be done with the right-hand first, second, and third fingers. The strum is done by starting with the fingers curled and while strumming across the strings, straightening them. The strum is a combination of the fingers, the wrist, and the elbow. The alternating bass patterns may also be done with a pick. Be sure to pick and strum the strings straight down. After picking the sixth string, the sixth string may be included in the strum, or only five strings may be strummed.

Practice the following exercise using the alternating bass pattern for 6-string chords. If the measure is blank, continue the pattern.

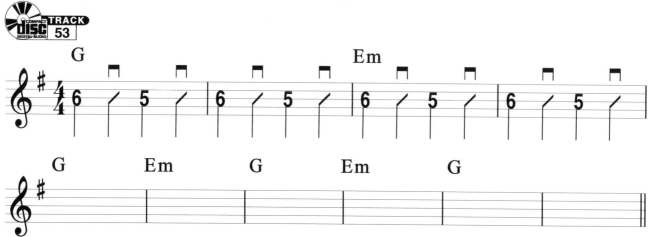

64

The pattern for one measure of a 5-string chord (like C) is written below. As with the 6-string pattern, this can be done with the fingers or a pick. After picking the fifth string, four strings may be strummed or the fifth string can be included in the strum. Hold any 5-string chord and practice this pattern.

Practice the following using the 5-string alternating bass pattern. Continue playing the pattern in the blank measures.

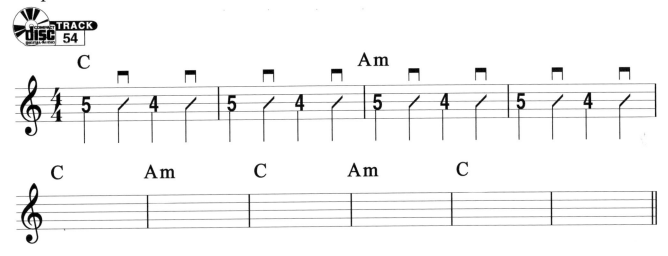

The alternating bass pattern for one measure of a 4-string chord in 4/4 is shown below. Practice the following using the 4-string, 5-string alternating bass patterns.

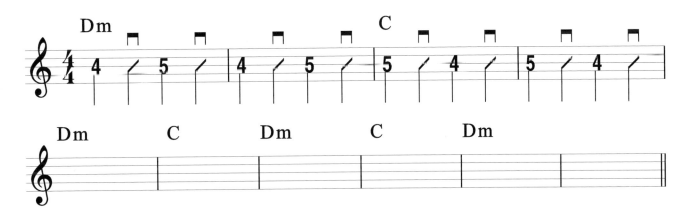

Practice the following exercise using alternating bass patterns for 6-string, 5-string, and 4-string chords. As reminders, the patterns are written above some of the measures. Depending on whether the chord is a 6-, 5-, or 4-string chord, play the appropriate patterns in the blank measures.

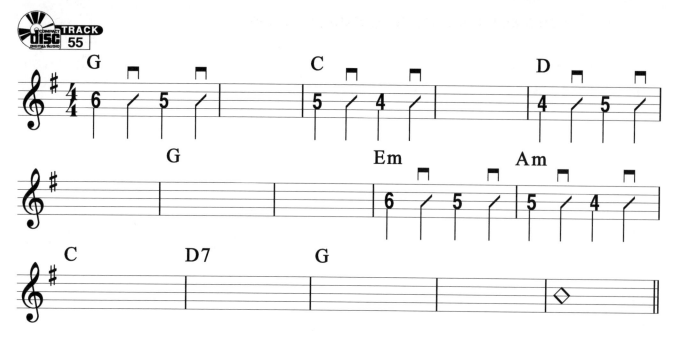

A variation of the alternating bass pattern for one measure of a 6-string chord is shown below. Notice, the picking of the fifth string on the third beat has been replaced with picking the fourth string.

Practice the following exercise using the 6-string variation.

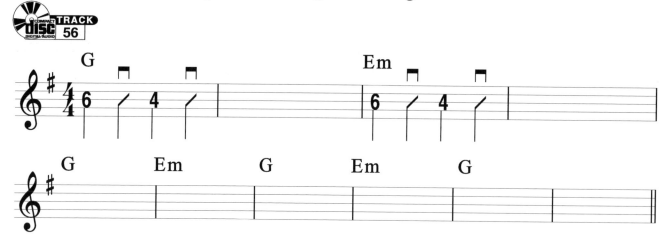

A variation of the 5-string chord pattern for 4/4 is shown below. The fourth string has been replaced with the picking of the sixth string. If the 5-string C chord is played using this variation, after playing the ⁵, the left hand third finger is moved to the sixth string, third fret to play the ⁶.

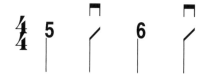

Practice the following using the 5-string variation.

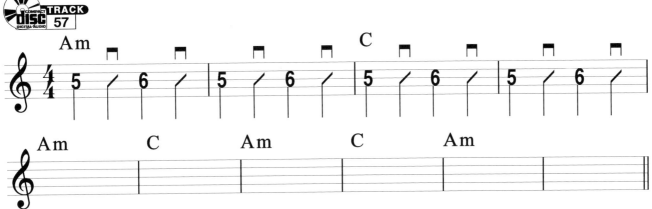

The patterns will not be written in the music, so…when applying the alternating bass patterns to a song in 4/4, determine if the chord for the measure is a 6-, 5-, or 4-string chord. Then, apply the appropriate pattern for that chord. Remember, each pattern takes one measure of 4/4 to complete. For the 6- and 5-string chords, the basic alternating bass pattern or the variations of the pattern may be used.

Practice the following songs using alternating bass for 4/4. As a reminder, patterns have been written above some of the measures.

WILL THE CIRCLE BE UNBROKEN

If two chords appear in a measure, play the first half of each chord's pattern as shown below:

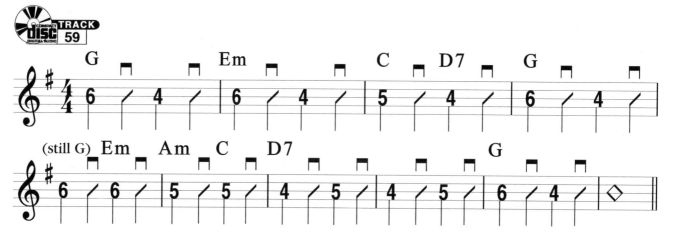

Play the following songs using alternating bass accompaniment.

SHE'LL BE COMIN' 'ROUND THE MOUNTAIN

Anonymous

JINGLE BELLS

Alternating Bass For 3/4

The alternating bass patterns for one measure of the 6-, 5-, and 4-strings chords in 3/4 are shown below. The lowest note of the chord is picked, followed by two strums. Each pattern takes one measure of 3/4 to complete.

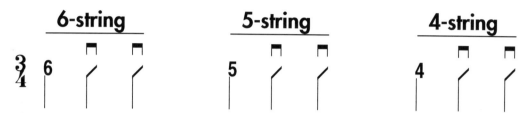

Practice the following progression using the alternating bass for 3/4. The patterns have been written in the first measure of each chord. In the blank measures, play the appropriate pattern.

In 3/4, if the same chord is repeated for more than one measure, the bass can alternate as shown below.

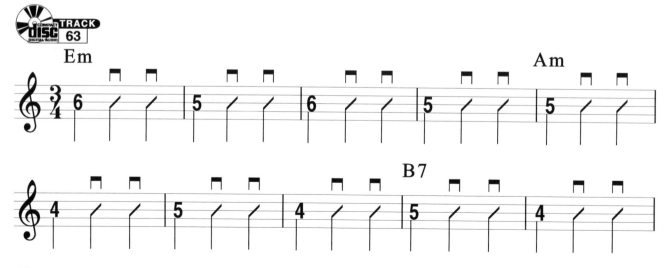

Practice the following songs in 3/4 using alternating bass.

After playing these songs, go to songs in 3/4 that appeared earlier in this book and apply the alternating bass accompaniment.

HOME ON THE RANGE

MY WILD IRISH ROSE

Words and Music by
Chauncy Olcott

MY BONNIE LIES OVER THE OCEAN

H. J. Fulmer

The F Chord

The F chord is drawn on the diagram below. The challenge with this chord is to get the first finger of the left hand to lay across strings one and two in the first fret. The loop above the strings indicates the finger is barred across strings one and two. It may be helpful if the left-hand thumb is brought a bit lower on the neck, so the first joint of the left-hand first finger can remain more flat.

Practice until you get a clear sound on each string. Then, play the exercise and song that follow. Use strum patterns or alternating bass patterns. When using the alternating bass for 4/4, with the F chord, play the 4 ⁄. Then, move the left-hand third finger to the fifth string, third fret to play the 5 ⁄.

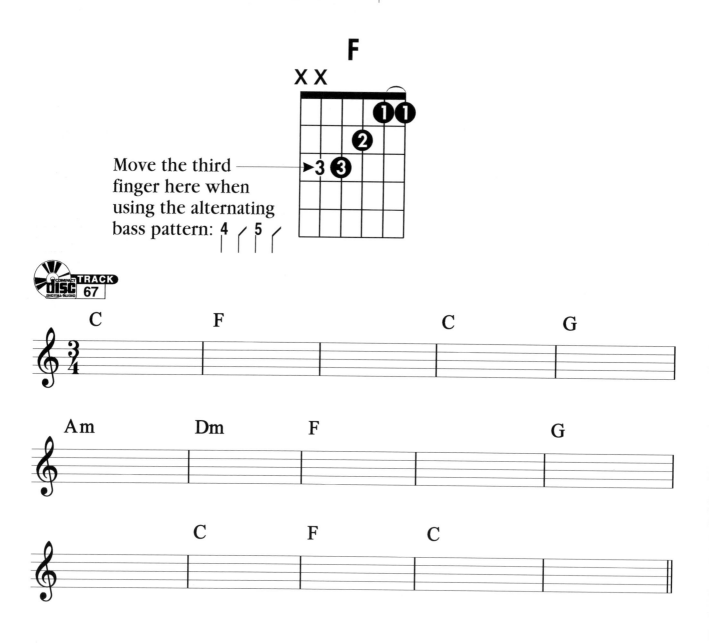

MR. BOJANGLES

Words and Music by
Jerry Jeff Walker

1. I knew a man, Bo - jan-gles, and he danced for you in worn out shoes, with sil - ver hair, a rag-ged shirt and bag - gy pants, the old soft shoe. He jumped so high, jumped so high, then he light - ly touched down. Mis - ter Bo - jan - gles, Mis-ter Bo - jan - gles, Mis - ter Bo - jan - gles, dance.

2. *See additional lyrics.*

2. I met him in a cell in New Orleans
   I was down and out.
   He looked at me to be the eyes of age,
   As he spoke right out.
   He talked of life,
   Talked of life.
   He laughed, slapped his leg a step.
   Mr. Bojangles, (etc.)

3. He said his name, Bojangles,
   Then he danced a lick across the cell.
   He grabbed his pants a better stance,
   Oh, he jumped up high.
   He clicked his heels.
   He let go a laugh, let go a laugh,
   Shook back his clothes all around.
   Mr. Bojangles, (etc.)

3. He danced for those at minstrel shows
   And county fairs throughout the South.
   He spoke with tears of fifteen years
   How his dog and he traveled about.
   His dog up and died,
   He up and died,
   After twenty years he still grieves.
   Mr. Bojangles, (etc.)

4. He said, "I dance now at ev'ry chance
   In honky tonks for drinks and tips.
   But most of the time I spend
   Behind these county bars,"
   He said, "I drinks a bit."
   He shook his head and as he shook his head,
   I heard someone ask please,
   Mr. Bojangles, (etc.)

Fingerstyle

"Fingerstyle playing" means playing the strings with the right-hand thumb and fingers, rather than using a pick. Before playing fingerstyle, an understanding of right-hand position and type of strokes is necessary. In the illustration below, the right-hand thumb is to the left of the fingers (when viewed from the top). The thumb is extended and the right-hand fingers are curled. The wrist is bent slightly. To put the right-hand in position, rest the thumb on the fifth string, the index finger on the third string, the middle finger on the second string, and the ring finger on the first string.

In fingerstyle playing, there are two types of motion used to stroke the strings...free stroke and rest stroke. The free stroke is used to play fingerpicking accompaniment patterns, and the rest stroke is often used when playing single note passages. Free stroke and rest stroke are illustrated and described below.

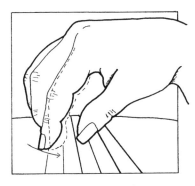

Figure 1

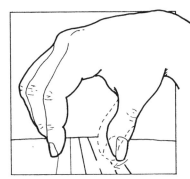

Figure 2

Rest Stroke

The rest stroke is commonly used to play melodies and is popular in solo guitar playing. To do the rest stroke, the flesh on the tip of the finger strokes the string is an upward (not outward) motion. The nail strokes the string as it passes by. The finger then comes to rest on the *next string* (see figure 1). The first joint of the finger (the one closest to the nail) should not bend. The second and third joints are active and should bend.

The thumb rest stroke is done by moving the thumb downward and playing the string with the tip of the thumb and the nail. The thumb then comes to rest on the next string down (see figure 2).

Practice playing the open sixth string several times using the rest stroke with the thumb. Then, practice playing the open fifth and fourth strings.

After playing the open bass strings with the thumb using the rest stroke, practice playing then third string open with the right-hand index finger using the rest stroke. Finally, use the rest stroke and play the first string open with the right-hand third finger.

Free Stroke

This is the stroke which is commonly used in accompaniment-style fingerpicking. Because it allows the strings to ring, it is good for fingerpicking. It may also be used to play single note melodies. To do the free stroke, the finger picks the string and then is pulled out slightly to avoid touching the next string. Remember, it barely misses the next string. Do not pull away from the guitar too far or the string will slap (see figure 3). As with the rest stroke, when using a free stroke, the first joint should not bend. This first joint acts like a shock absorber. The second and third joints are the active joints.

The free stroke with the thumb is similar. After the thumb strokes the string, it is moved slightly outward to avoid hitting the next string (see figure 4).

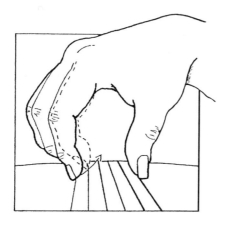

Figure 3

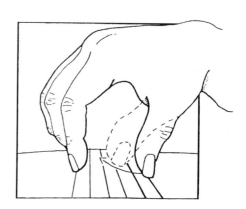

Figure 4

All the fingerpicking patterns and exercises in this section of the book should be done using the free stroke.

The following exercises will develop right-hand coordination which will be helpful in learning fingerpicking patterns. Repeat each exercise several times.

In the following exercises, the numbers written indicate the strings which are to be played (1= 1st string, 2= 2nd string, etc.). The letters, written to the side of the numbers, indicate which right-hand finger is to pick the string.

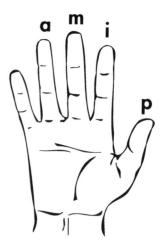

Right Hand

Right hand:		
p	=	**pulgar** (thumb)
i	=	**indice** (index finger)
m	=	**media** (middle finger)
a	=	**anular** (third finger)

In the first exercise, the index finger rests on the 3rd string (touches, but does not play), the middle finger rests on the 2nd string, and the ring finger rests on the 1st string. While the fingers rest on strings one, two, and three, the thumb plays the 6th string open using a free stroke. In all of the exercises below, the strings are played using a free stroke. The stem below each number indicates that each stroke gets one beat.

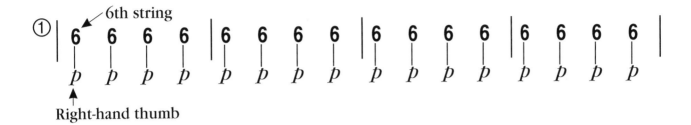

In the next exercises, the thumb rests on the sixth string, while the fingers play strings one, two, and three open.

Next, the thumb plays the sixth string at the same time as the fingers play the top strings.

In exercise #4, the thumb alternates with the fingers

In exercise #5, the thumb plays the 6th string, followed by the index finger playing the 3rd string, the middle finger playing the 2nd string, and the third finger playing the 1st string. The stems under the numbers serve the same purpose as stems on notes. Stems connected with a single beam indicate two strokes (strings picked) per beat (eighth notes). The brackets indicate measures. Each pattern take one, 4/4 measure to complete. The right-hand fingering is written below the string numbers.

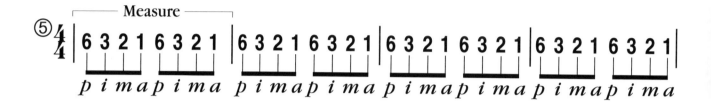

Exercise #6 has the finger order as pami, pami, and the string order as 6123, 6123.

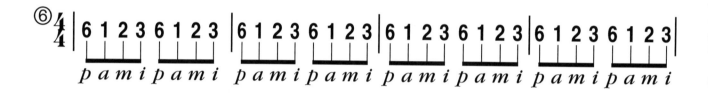

Fingerpicking Patterns

A fingerpicking pattern which could be used to play songs in 4/4 time is written below. This pattern is for one measure of a 6-string chord in 4/4. Remember, a 6-string chord is one which, when strummed, all six strings are played. Examples of 6-string chords would include G and Em.

The numbers in the pattern below represent strings to be picked. Letters under the numbers show which right-hand fingers are used to pick the string. The rhythm of the pattern is indicated by the stems under the numbers. Hold a G chord and practice this pattern.

6-String Chords (ex. G and Em)

$$\frac{4}{4} \mid 6 \quad 4 \quad 3 \quad 2 \quad 6 \quad 4 \quad 3 \quad 2 \leftarrow \text{Strings}$$

p	*p*	*i*	*m*	*p*	*p*	*i*	*m* ◄——Right-hand fingers
1	&	2	&	3	&	4	& ◄——Rhythm

This fingerpicking pattern is sometimes called an "arpeggio-pattern." Arpeggio means "broken chord." In this fingerpicking pattern the chord is "broken" and the strings are played one at a time. This pattern works well with slow songs in 4/4.

The pattern for one measure of a 5-string chord is written below. Notice the right-hand finger order is the same as the pattern for 6-string chords.

In accompaniment style fingerpicking, it is common for the right-hand finger order to remain the same even though the string order may vary.

5-String Chords (ex. C and Am)

$$\frac{4}{4} \mid 5 \quad 4 \quad 3 \quad 2 \quad 5 \quad 4 \quad 3 \quad 2 \mid$$

p	*p*	*i*	*m*	*p*	*p*	*i*	*m*
1	&	2	&	3	&	4	&

The arpeggio fingerpick pattern for one measure of a 4-string chord is written below.

4-String Chords (ex. D and F)

$$\frac{4}{4} \mid 4 \quad 3 \quad 2 \quad 1 \quad 4 \quad 3 \quad 2 \quad 1 \mid$$

p	*p*	*i*	*m*	*p*	*p*	*i*	*m*
1	&	2	&	3	&	4	&

To apply this fingerpick pattern to accompany a song, determine if the chord for the measure is 6-, 5-, or 4-string chord, and then play the appropriate pattern for that chord.

Practice the following exercises using the arpeggio fingerpicking pattern. As a guide, the patterns have been written in some of the measures. In the empty measures, play the appropriate pattern for that chord.

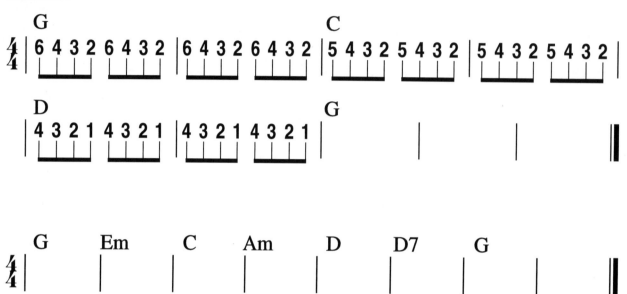

If two chords appear in a measure, half of the pattern is played on each chord.

Practice the following song using the arpeggio fingerpicking pattern. As a help, patterns have been written above some of the measures. Don't be concerned with playing the melody notes. Focus on playing the correct fingerpick pattern.

THE WATER IS WIDE

Fingerpicking 3/4 Time

This section contains several fingerpicking patterns which work for 3/4 time. The first pattern is similar to the arpeggio fingerpick pattern. The patterns for one measure of the 6-, 5-, and 4-string chords are shown below. The right-hand finger order is written under the string numbers in the 6-string pattern. The same right-hand finger order is used to play each pattern (6-, 5-, and 4-string chords). The rhythm is written under the pattern for the 5-string chords. The rhythm which is played on the 5-string chords is also played on the 6- and 4-string chords.

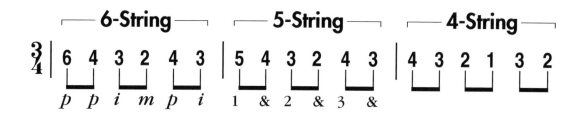

Practice the following exercise using the fingerpick pattern for 3/4.

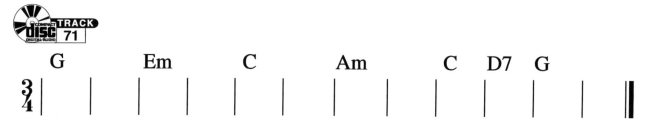

Practice the following song using the fingerpick pattern for 3/4.

SCARBOROUGH FAIR

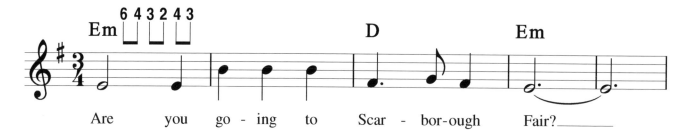

Are you go - ing to Scar - bor-ough Fair?_____

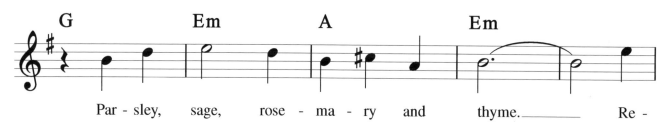

Par - sley, sage, rose - ma - ry and thyme._____ Re -

84

mem - ber   me   to   one   who   lives   there,

She   once   was   a   true   love   of   mine.

The next fingerpick pattern for 3/4 is only slightly different from the first 3/4 pattern presented. In this pattern, on the first beat of each measure, two strings are played together. The lower string is played with the thumb, and the 1st string is played with the right-hand middle finger. Hold any 6-,5-, or 4-string chords and practice this pattern.

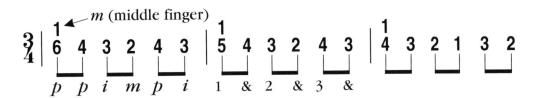

Practice the following exercise and song using this fingerpick pattern. Repeat the pattern in the blank measures.

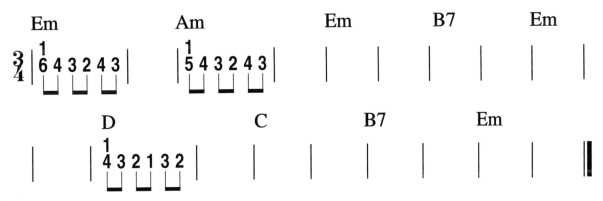

SILENT NIGHT

Franz Grüber

Gently

Si - lent night, ho - ly night,

All is calm, all is bright. Round yon

vir - gin moth - er and child. Ho - ly in - fant so

ten - der and mild. Sleep in heav - en - ly

peace. _____ Sleep ___ in heav - en - ly peace. _____

Written below is another fingerpick style which works well when playing songs in 3/4 time. The pattern for one measure of a 6-string chord is written on the left. The pattern for one measure of a 5-string chord is written in the middle and the pattern for one measure of a 4-string chord is written on the right.

In this style, when two strings are played together, the right-hand index finger (i) plays the lower (larger) string, and the right-hand middle finger (m) plays the higher (smaller) string. After practicing this new 3/4 fingerpick style holding various 6-, 5-, and 4-string chords, practice using this style to play some of the previous songs and exercises in this book which are 3/4.

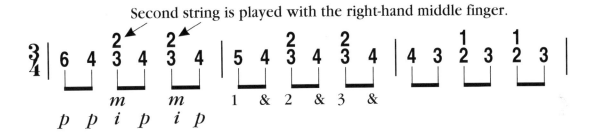

The fingerpick patterns for 3/4 may be played using "swing rhythm." Remember, in swing rhythm, each beat is divided into a one-short pattern rather than divided evenly. Each beat sounds like an eighth note triplet (♪♪♪) with the middle note tied (♪♪♪). One of the 3/4 fingerpick patterns for 3/4 is shown below with swing rhythm.

$$\frac{3}{4} \mid \text{6-4} \quad \text{3-2} \quad \text{4-3} \mid$$

count: 1   la   2   la   3   la

Practice the previous 3/4 songs and exercises in this section of the book, only now use swing rhythm.

Travis Fingerpick Style

One of the more popular fingerpick patterns used to play music in 4/4 time is called "Travis picking." This style is named after the great country guitarist, Merle Travis. One of the characteristics of Merle Travis's technique was the thumb alternating between two bass strings. The right-hand thumb would play on the first of each beat. The right-hand fingers would play between the thumb strokes. The Travis fingerpick patterns for one measure of 6-string, 5-string, and 4-string chords are shown below. The right-hand finger order is written under the 6-string pattern, and the rhythm is written below the 5-string pattern. The same right-hand finger order and rhythm is used for each pattern. Hold G for the 6-string chord, C for the 5-string chord, and D7 for the 4-string chord, and play the following patterns.

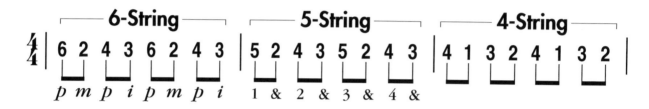

Practice the following exercise using the Travis fingerpick style. In the blank measures, play the appropriate 6-, 5-, or 4-string pattern for the chord.

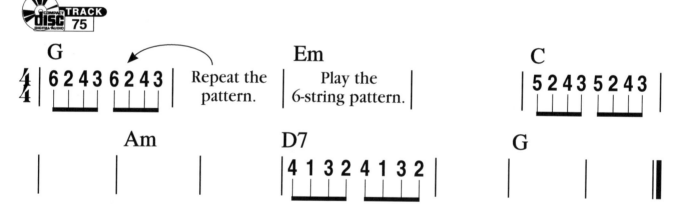

Practice the following songs using the Travis fingerpick style.

A POOR WAYFARING STRANGER

Traditional

I'm just a   poor,_____way-far-ing   strang-er_____   a - trav-lin'

88

WORRIED MAN BLUES

Traditional

It takes a wor - ried man to sing a wor - ried

song. It takes a wor - ried, wor - ried man to sing a wor - ried

song. It takes a wor - ried man to sing a wor - ried

song. I'm wor - ried now, but I won't be wor - ried long.

A variation of the Travis style is written below. It is similar to the Travis pattern previously presented. However, the string which was picked on the "and" of the first beat has been omitted. Hold G, C, and D7 chords and practice this variation.

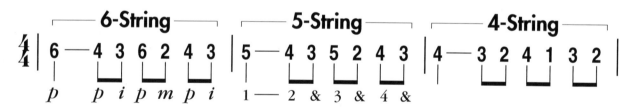

Practice the next exercise using the variation of the Travis pick.

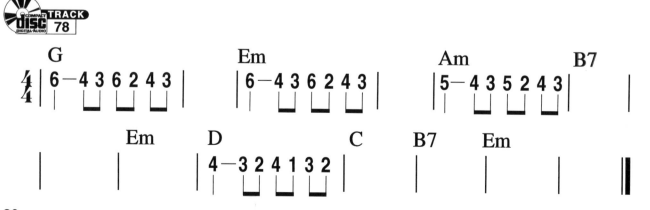

Practice the following songs using the Travis variation.

BABY DON'T LOVE ME

I love my ba-by,— but my ba-by don't love—me.

I love my ba-by,— but my ba-by don't love—me.

Feel-in' down and lone-ly,— Wish these blues would set me — free.

YOU'RE THE CURE

Help a sick man ba-by.— Won't you help me please?

Help a sick man ba-by.— Won't you help— me please?

All I need's your lov-in'.— You're the cure for my dis-ease.

Solo Guitar Playing

The material presented in the following sections of this book will enable you to play solo guitar by playing single note melodies. The right-hand thumb or a pick should be used to play the material in this section of the book.

Tablature

One method of writing music for guitar is called tablature. In tablature, the horizontal lines represent the guitar strings. The first string is on the top. The numbers on the lines indicate in which fret to place the left-hand fingers. The number of the left-hand finger being used should be the same as the fret number.

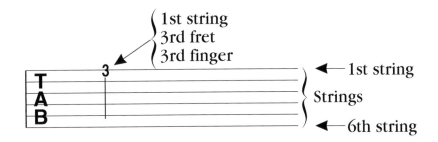

In the next example, the left-hand second finger is placed on the first string in the second fret.

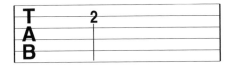

Time values are written with stems and/or circled numbers. The chart below shows some of the various time values.

3 = One stem under or above the number = 1 beat.

(3) = Circled number with a stem = 2 beats. Play the string on the first beat and let it ring through the second beat.

(3)· = Circled number with a dot = 3 beats.

(3) = Circled number = 4 beats.

If numbers are written on top of one another, the strings are played at the same time. A zero indicates an open string. The following shows how a G chord would be written.

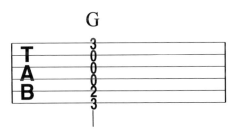

Practice the following tunes written in tablature and using the notes on the first two strings. Use the right-hand thumb or a pick to play the single strings.

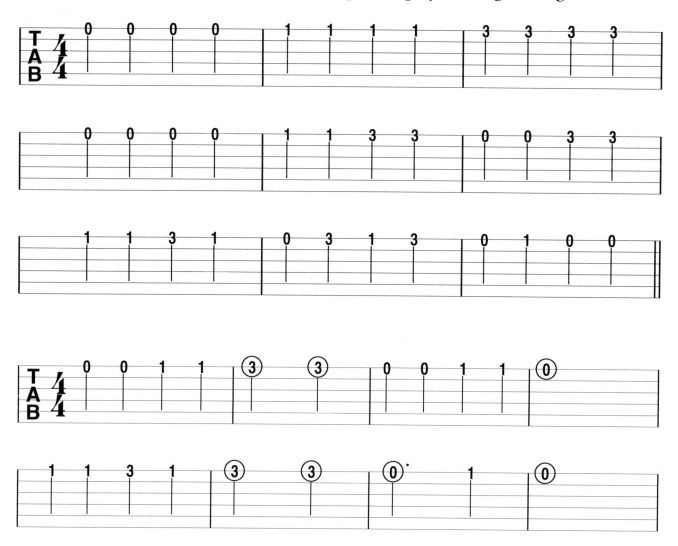

Play the following song written in tablature. The chords written above the measures are for another guitarist to play the accompaniment. If you are playing the tablature, ignore the chords.

SONG OF JOY

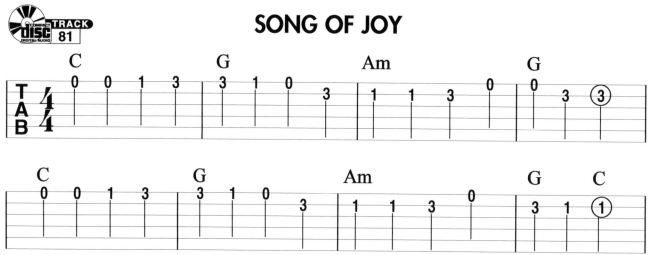

Play the following on the second string using tablature.

```
T  4  0   0   0   0 | 1   1   1   1 | 0   0   0   0 | 3   3   3   3
A  4                |               |               |
B  4                |               |               |
```

```
   0   0   1   1 | 0   0   3   3 | 1   3   1   3 | 0   0   1   0
                 |               |               |
                 |               |               |
```

Reading Standard Notation

This section of the book presents the tools necessary for reading standard notation (notes). Shown below are the staff, clef, parts of a note, and the time values of the notes. All of the music for guitar in this book will be written in treble clef.

 **Staff:** Consisting of five lines and four spaces. Each line and space has a name with a letter in the alphabet.

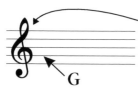 **Treble Clef (or G Clef):** Indicates that the second line from the bottom is named G. Most guitar music is written in the treble clef.

Names of the lines and spaces of the staff (treble clef)

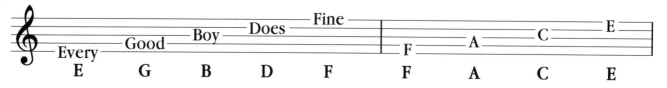

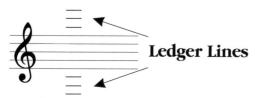 **Ledger Lines**

 Note: Each note assumes the name of the line or space of the staff on which it appears. The stem may go up or down.

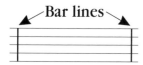 **Bar Line:** The vertical lines separating sections of the staff.

 **Measure:** The space between the bar lines.

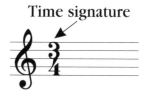 **Time Signature:** The top number indicates the number of beats per measure. The bottom number indicates what type of note gets one beat. In this case, a quarter note would get one beat and there would be three beats in each measure.

 The C written after the treble clef indicates 4/4 (common time).

Time Values

Written below are the time values of some of the notes and rests. If a rest is written, do not play or let the previous note ring. These time values are given assuming that the bottom number of the time signature is a four ($\frac{4}{4}$). The quarter note would get the basic unit or one beat. If the bottom number of the time signature is a eight, the values double.

NAME		TIME VALUE
♩ =	Quarter note	1 beat
♩ =	Half note. Play the note on the 1st beat and let it sound through the 2nd beat.	2 beats
♩. =	Dotted half note. The dot increases the length of the note by 1/2 its original time value.	3 beats
𝅝 =	Whole note	4 beats
𝄽 =	Quarter rest	1 beat
▬ =	Half rest	2 beats
▬ =	Whole rest	4 beats

Shown on the following pages are the notes on strings one and two. Written above each note is the name of the note and written below the note is the fret placement. Remember, open means that no left-hand fingers are pushing on the strings. The left-hand finger used to push on the string should match the fret number in which it is pressing.

Notes On The First String

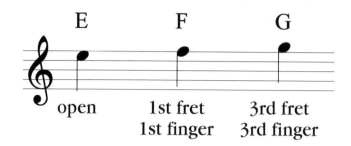

Practice the following exercises using the notes on the first string.

Notes on the Second String

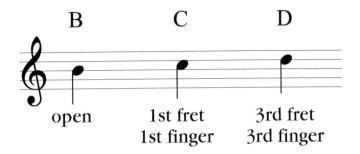

Practice the following exercises using the notes on the second string.

The following songs use the notes on strings one and two.

The chords written above the measures may be played by another guitarist as an accompaniment. If you are playing the notes, do not be concerned with the chords.

MERRILY WE ROLL ALONG

SONG OF JOY

Notes on the Third String

Written below are the notes on the third string.

G   A

open   2nd fret
         2nd finger

Practice the following exercise using the notes on the third string.

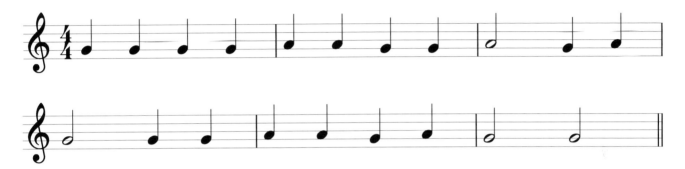

Practice the following songs using the notes on the first three strings.

A SEPARATE PEACE

TRACK 86

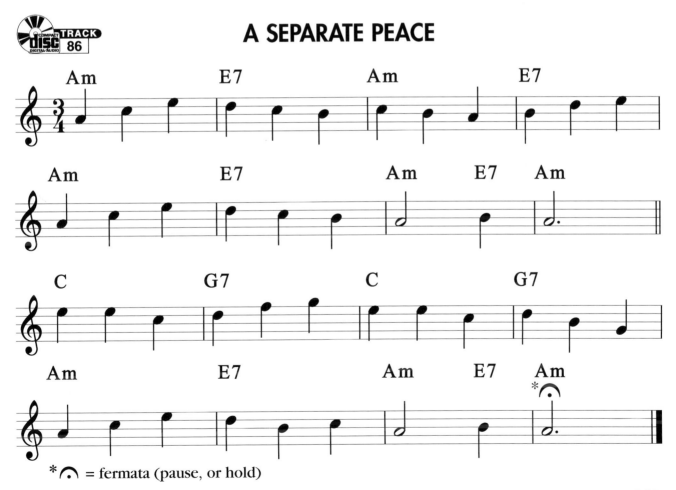

* ⌢ = fermata (pause, or hold)

WHEN THE SAINTS GO MARCHING IN

If a song begins with an incomplete measure,
then these are called "pick-up notes."
The missing beat is in the last measure.

Count: (1)   2   3   4

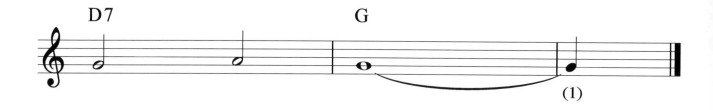

(1)

Four-String Tablature

The following exercises and tunes are written in tablature and use the first four strings. Remember, use the same left-hand finger number as the fret number.

SCARBOROUGH FAIR

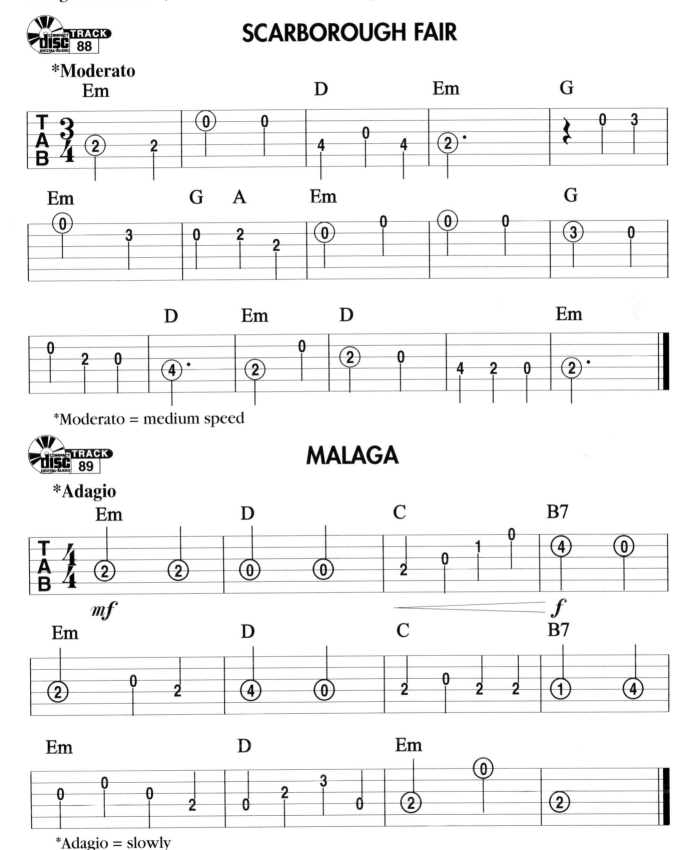

*Moderato = medium speed

MALAGA

*Adagio = slowly

Notes On The Fourth String

Shown below are the notes on the fourth string. Practice the exercise using the notes on the fourth string only, and then play the solo that combines the notes on the first four strings.

A POOR WAYFARING STRANGER

A loop that connects two same notes together is called a tie. When two notes are connected with a tie, play the first note and let it ring through the time value of the second note. Do not play the second note.

HUNGARIAN DANCE #4

* These are first and second endings. The first time through, play the music under the first ending ([1.]). Then, repeat at the repeat sign. The second time through skip the music under the first ending and play the music under the second ending ([2.]).

Sharps and Naturals

This, ♯, is a sharp sign. When it appears in front of a note, the note is played one half step (one fret) higher. Be sure that the left-hand finger number used to depress the string is the same as the fret number in which it is placed.

If an open string is sharp, it is played in the first fret. When a sharp sign appears in front of a note, it will affect all of the same notes until the end of the measure. After the bar line, the sharp is cancelled.

This, ♮, is a natural sign. When it appears in front of a note, it cancels a sharp or flat.

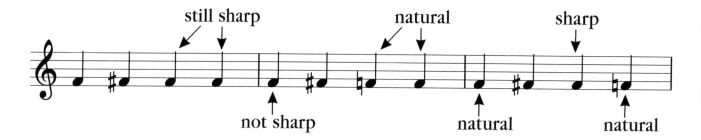

Play the following piece which uses the notes on the first four strings and contains some sharps. Remember, if the third string, open (G) is sharp, it will be played on the third string, in the first fret (with the first finger).

GREENSLEEVES

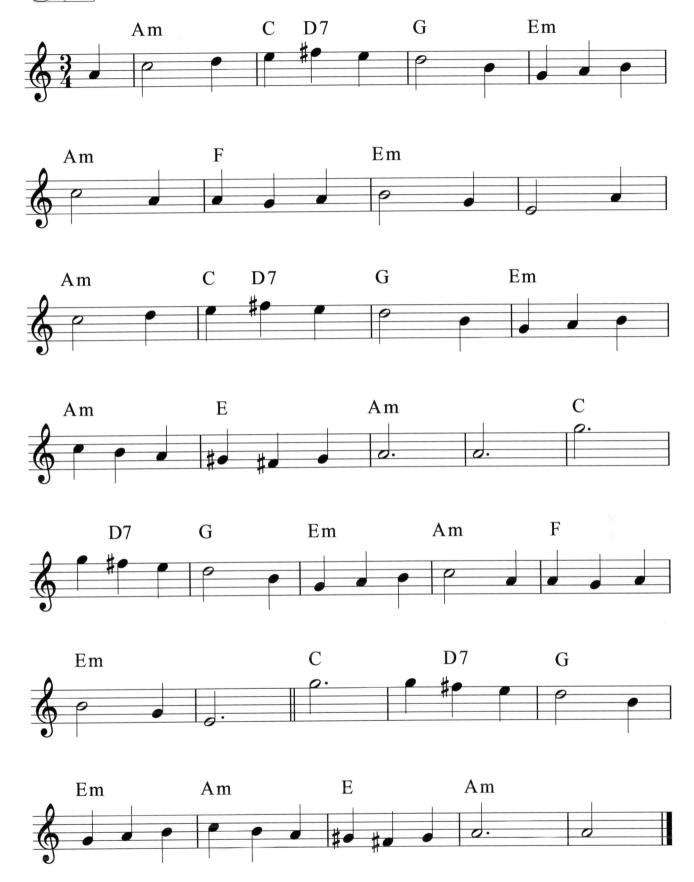

More Tablature

Practice the following tunes written in tablature using all six strings.

WALKIN' BLUES

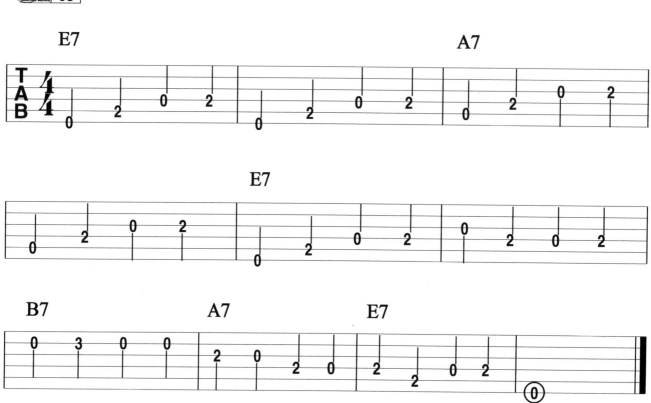

Notes on the Fifth String

The notes on the fifth string are shown below.

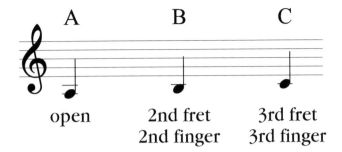

A
open

B
2nd fret
2nd finger

C
3rd fret
3rd finger

The next exercise uses only the notes on the fifth string.

Notes On The Sixth String

The notes on the sixth string are shown below.

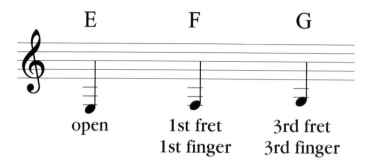

The next exercise uses only the notes on the sixth string.

Play the following piece that emphasizes the notes on strings five and six.

TRACK 95

HOUSE OF THE RISING SUN

Flats

This is a flat sign: ♭. When it appears in front of a note, the note is to be played one half step (one fret) lower (towards the head of the guitar). Be sure that the left-hand finger number used to depress the string is the same as the fret number. As with sharps, the flat will affect all of the same notes that follow in that measure. A bar line and/or a natural sign will cancel a flat.

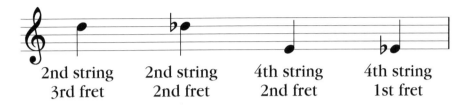

2nd string	2nd string	4th string	4th string
3rd fret	2nd fret	2nd fret	1st fret

If an open string is flat, go to the next largest string and find the fret where that string sounds the same as the open string. Then, lower the note 1/2 step (one fret). Be sure to use the same number left-hand finger as the fret number.

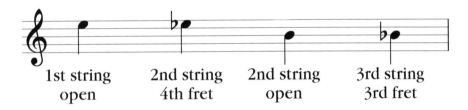

1st string	2nd string	2nd string	3rd string
open	4th fret	open	3rd fret

Play the following tune containing flats.

KLEZMER TUNE

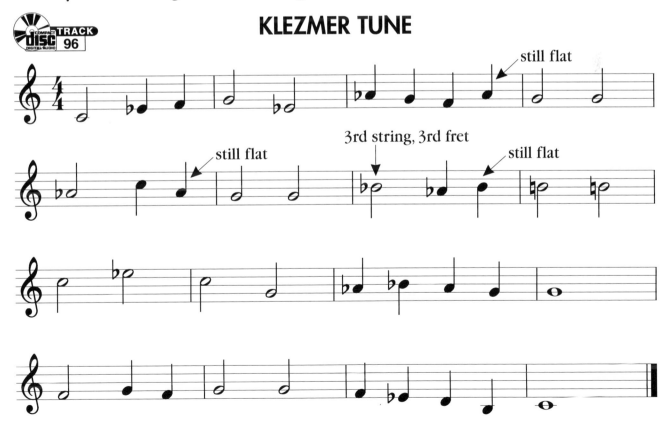

Key Signatures

When sharp or flat appear at the beginning of the music next to the clef sign, it is called a *key signature*.

Throughout the rest of the piece, all of the notes that have letter names corresponding to the names of the sharps or flats in the key signature will be sharp or flat. A natural sign can be used to cancel a sharp or flat from the key signature.

Practice the following tunes and pay close attention to the notes affected by the key signature.

O COME, O COME EMMANUEL

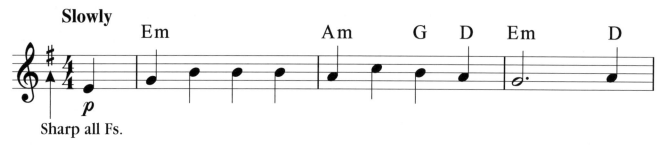

Sharp all Fs.

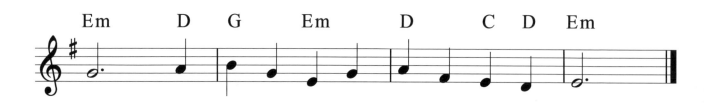

WALTZ

See p.116 for the finger-ing of the C7 chord.

TWILIGHT

Sharp all of the Fs and Cs

Flat all of the Bs

The Capo

The capo is a clamp that can be fastened on the neck of the guitar to raise the pitch of the strings. The farther up the neck the capo is placed, the higher the pitch. To use a capo, clamp it next to the desired fret. Finger the chords as if the first fret up the neck from the capo were the first fret on the guitar. The chord finger patterns will still be the same, but the pitches of the chords will be higher.

The use of the capo changes the key. However, the same chord fingerings are still used. Imagine that the first fret up the neck from the capo is the first fret on the guitar. The use of the capo may put songs in a key that is easier to sing. Each time the capo is moved up one fret, it raises the key (or pitch) 1/2 step. For example, when playing a G chord with the capo in the first fret, the chord actually sounds like a G$\sharp$ or A$\flat$ chord. You don't need be concerned with the actual pitch, unless you are playing with another instrument.

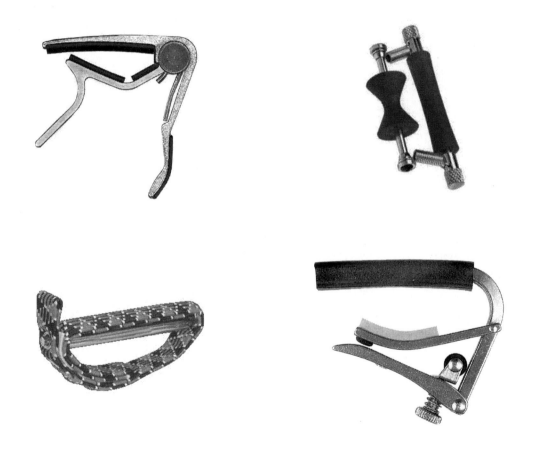

Chords

Major Chords

A
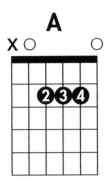

B♭
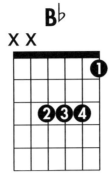

B
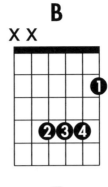

C
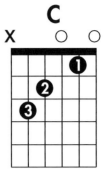

D
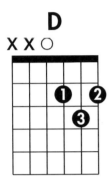

E
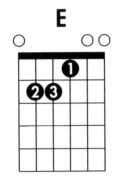

F
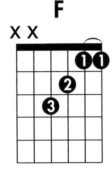

G
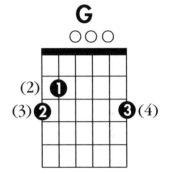

Minor Chords

Am
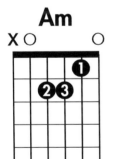

Bm
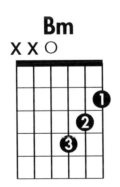

Cm
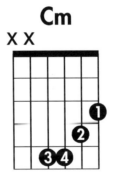

Dm
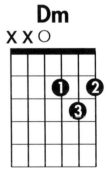

Em
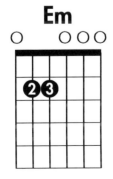

Fm
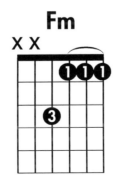

Gm
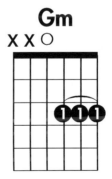

Seventh Chords

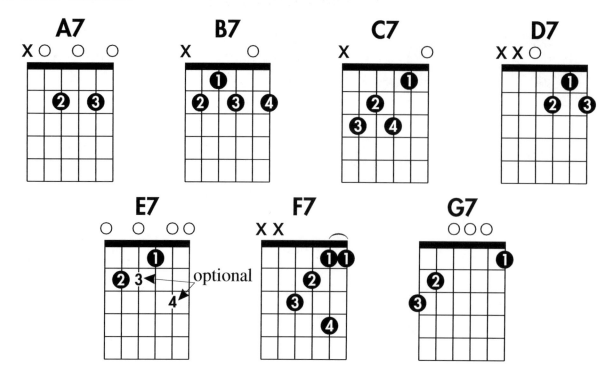

Minor Seventh Chords

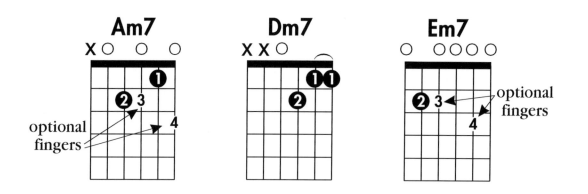

Major Seventh Chords

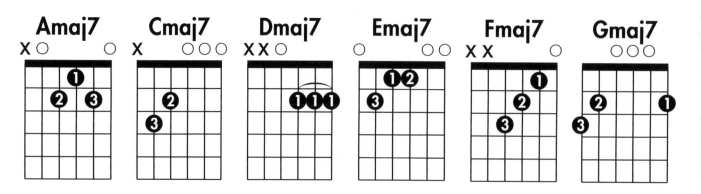

Mike Christiansen

Mike Christiansen is a Professor of Music and Director of Guitar Studies in the Music Department at Utah State University. In 1994, Mike was selected as Professor Of The Year at Utah State University. Mike received the ASTA (American String Teachers Association) Utah Chapter Outstanding Collegiate Educator of the Year Award in 2006. In 2007, Mike received the Utah State University Artist of the Year award and the Overall Scholar of the Year Award for the College of Humanities Arts and Social Sciences. He has taught workshops at many schools and is a frequent clinician for guitarists and educators at various conferences. He averages over 130 performances annually as a soloist, with the group, *Mirage,* and with the *Lightwood Duo* (a clarinet-guitar duo that has released six recordings). Mike is the author and/or co-author of 42 books. He has recorded 29 CDs, and appears on 21 instructional videos. Mike has had articles published in several magazines including *Just Jazz Guitar, Acoustic Guitar, Fingerstyle,* and *Soundboard,* and has been a back-up musician for various artists and has recorded music for television and films.

EXCELLENCE IN MUSIC

MEL BAY®

Since 1947

Made in the USA
Las Vegas, NV
09 April 2021